THE SELF-CONCEPT
OF
BLACK AMERICANS

Vivian Verdell Gordon
Assistant Professor, Sociology
Chairperson, Afro-American
and African Studies
University of Virginia

University Press
of America™

ACKNOWLEDGMENTS

I wish to express my appreciation for the assistance,
encouragement and support of several of my present and
former colleagues: Theodore Caplow, Charles Green,
Dave Bromley, Charles Longino and Jeanne Biggar. Without
their wise counsel, I surely would have floundered more
than I did throughout this venture.

Special appreciation goes to Bruce Busching, who is both
a scientist and an excellent teacher, for his willingness
to marshal his resources and spend numerous hours with me
tutoring and critiqueing both my thinking and my work. He .
continues to believe that one day I will be a scientist.

Dedicated to:

My parents,

     Susie and Thomas Verdell

and

My family,

     Ronald, Ronnie and Susan

With love and appreciation for their support and patience.

INTRODUCTION

This work presents an analysis of empirical studies which have been concerned with the self-concept of Black Americans in the past 35 years. The information and discussions attempt to answer three questions: (1) What has been the historical background of Black self-concept research, (2) What are some of the methodological problems with the research, and (3) What are some directions in the theoretical orientation of the research.

Of particular interest to those who are concerned with the Sociology of Black America and generalized ethnic group studies will be the fact that there is no basis for the statement==so often stated as fact--that Blacks have low self-concepts. If we would follow the challenge presented by DuBois and echoed most recently by Ladner in <u>The Death of White Sociology</u>, sociological studies about Black Americans must be re-examined in terms of both theory and data to allow for a clear indication of points of departure in "traditional thought" with respect to specific ethnic and cultural groups. Black "personality theory" has been surrounded by debate and couched in myth. The data and discussions presented here clearly identify the areas of debate and debunk the myths.

TABLE OF CONTENTS

Page

"If one were to look only at the location
of blacks in various institutional struc-
tures, at the numerous disadvantages and
disprivileges which they face, it would
be hard not to conclude, as so many scho-
lars have done, that blacks should have
lower self-esteem. Yet the recent evidence casts doubt upon this conclusion.
A finding which flies so squarely in the
face of sound social psychological theory
must pique our curiosity and command our
attention."

Morris Rosenberg.
Black and White Self-Esteem.
Arnold M. and Caroline Rose
Monograph, American Socio-
logical Association.

CHAPTER I

A HISTORICAL REVIEW OF RESEARCH CONCERNED WITH
THE SELF-CONCEPT OF BLACK AMERICANS

In this Chapter we shall review a body of empirical
research which has been concerned with the self-concept of
Black Americans. In our review we shall attempt to answer
several general questions: (1) What has been the major
theoretical orientation which has influenced this research?
(2) How has the black experience in the United States been
reflected in the interpretation of the results of the research? (3) What has been the range of the research, in
terms of the time frames of the studies, the methodologies,
the selection of respondents and the general findings and
conclusions?

To answer these and related questions, we shall
first briefly review the works which have provided the
theoretical orientation for social-psychological self-concept research. With these orientations in mind, we shall
review, also briefly, the black experience in the United
States, with particular attention to the conditions of
slavery, which appear frequently to be perceived by researchers in this area as the key factor in the overall
development of the black personality.

Social psychology began its focus upon the empirical study of the black self-concept in the middle 1930's. Prior to this time, studies giving attention to this issue were primarily theoretical. The studies presented here will be reviewed within the time frame 1939-1973. The latter part of the Chapter reports an extensive body of research, and studies have been grouped into three time periods of four- teen years (1939-1953), ten years (1954-1963), and ten years (1964-1973). These time frames allow for three relatively equal distributions of the total time period and will be used to divide studies for discussion throughout the dis- sertation. Within the time frames, the concluding summary table at the end of the chapter, reports: (1) the date of the research (2) the selection of respondents (3) the meth- odology and (4) the findings and conclusions, especially as this information may be categorized according to explicit or implicit statements about the black self-concept.

THE THEORETICAL ORIENTATION OF BLACK SELF-CONCEPT RESEARCH:

Early research on the self-concept of Black Americans focused upon the question of race awareness and identity formation and usually spoke about a generalized black personality. This foundation was derived largely from the works of Cooley and Mead, both of whom maintain that social interaction is the means by which an individual formulates his self-concept. C. H. Cooley stresses the importance of

the individual's perception of how others see him, and
introduces the concept of the looking-glass self.[1]

> Each to each a looking-glass
> Reflects the other that doth pass.

In explanation, he wrote:

> A self-idea of this sort seems to have three prin-
> cipal elements: the imagination of our appearance
> to the other person; the imagination of his judg-
> ment of that appearance; and some sort of self-
> feeling, such as pride or mortification . . . .
> The thing that moves us to pride or shame is not
> the mere mechanical reflection of ourselves, but
> an imputed sentiment, the imagined effect of this
> reflection upon another's mind . . . . We always
> imagine, and in imagining, share the judgments of
> the other mind.[2]

Of particular relevance is Cooley's thought that

> . . . the object of self-feeling is affected by
> the general course of history, by the particular
> development of nations, classes, and professions,
> and other conditions of this sort.[3]

George H. Mead[4] makes a similar argument about the
genesis of the self:

> . . . the individual experiences himself as such,
> not directly, but only indirectly, from the par-
> ticular standpoints of other individual members
> of the same social group, or from the generalized
> standpoint of the social group as a whole to which
> he belongs. For he enters his own experience as a
> self or individual, not directly or immediately,
> not by becoming a subject to himself, but only in

[1]Charles H. Cooley, Human Nature & The Social Order
(New York: Schocken Books, 1964).

[2]Ibid.

[3]Ibid.

[4]George H. Mead, Mind, Self, and Society (Chicago:
University of Chicago Press, 1934).

> so far as he first becomes an object to him-
> self just as other individuals are objects to
> him or in his experience; and he becomes an
> object to himself only by taking the attitudes
> of other individuals toward himself within a
> social environment or context of experience and
> behavior in which both he and they are invol-
> ved.[1]

On the question of the person's perception of the generalized other, Mead writes:

> . . . The organized community or social group
> which gives to the individual his unity of self may
> be called "the generalized other." The attitude of
> the generalized other is the attitude of the whole
> community.[2]

Mead, therefore, underscores the influence of the social
process upon the behavior and thought of individuals and
indicates that the conception of the individual self is de-
pendent upon that individual's reference to the generalized
other, or to salient others within the generalized other.
If these ideas of Cooley and Mead are correct, the history
of Black Americans becomes very relevant to considerations
of black self-concepts.

The history of blacks in America is a record of the
emergence of an oppressed people from conditions of slavery
as a moral-legal order to conditions of existence as a group
of low caste and class within the society.[3] Speaking to

---

[1]Ibid.

[2]Ibid.

[3]For a historical review of the development of racism
in America see: Knowles and Prewitt, eds., Institutionalized Racism in America; Kenneth Stamp, The Peculiar

the philosophy of the "inhuman" black American--Arnold A.
Sio reports:

> . . . slavery in the United States meant Negro
> slavery. In contrast to Latin American, slavery
> in the ante-bellum South involved "caste," "by
> law of nature," or "innate inferiority."[1]

Students of American history and particularly of the
history of the South are well aware that ". . . the conception of the slave as a racial inferior led to severe restrictions on manumission and to a low status for free Negroes."[1]
The color identity of the slave provided a unifying means
through which a people have come to be identified and grouped
as racially inferior and has provided the means for the
enforcement of legal measures which have helped to establish
and to maintain conditions of social and economic caste and
class.

To survive under such conditions, the black in
America often had to resort to a presentation of himself
which suggested docility, a lack of confidence and ability
(except for those skills which brought pride to his owner),
a child-like and entertaining manner, and other forms of
behavior which readily may be identified from an adjective

(Continued) Institution: Slavery in the Ante-Bellum South;
John H. Franklin, From Slavery to Freedom; Eugene Genovese,
The Political Economy of Slavery; and C. Van Woodward, The
Strange Career of Jim Crow.

[1]Sio, Arnold A. "Interpretations of Slavery: The
Slave Status in the Americas," in Structured Social Inequality
Celia S. Heller, ed. (New York: Hunter College Press, 1969).

check list for racial stereotyping as associated with the
black personality. (See Bayton, 1965).

On this same issue of the slave's presentation of
himself for his own safety and survival, Kenneth Stamp
writes:

> It was typical of an indulgent master not to take
> his slaves seriously but to look upon them as
> slightly comic figures . . . . Even the most sen-
> sitive master called adult slave men "boys" and
> women "girls" until in their old age he made them
> honorary "aunties" and "uncles".
>
> . . . Clearly, to enjoy the bounty of a paternal-
> istic master a slave had to give up all claims to
> respect as a responsible adult, all pretensions of
> independence. He had to understand the subtle et-
> iquette that governed his relations with his mas-
> ter: that fine line between friskiness and insub-
> ordination, between cuteness and insolence.[1]

It is against this background that the generalized
Negro personality, the black youth's racial awareness and
the self-concept of black Americans, is presumed to have
developed into negative self-evaluations. For example,
Lee Rainwater in explanation of the low self-esteem he
observed among lower class black families, writes:

> But in Negro slum culture growing up involves an
> ever-increasing appreciation of one's shortcomings,
> of the impossibility of finding a self-sufficient
> and gratifying way of living.
>
> . . . one of the effects of ghettoization is to
> mask the ultimate enemy so that the understanding
> of the fact of victimization by a caste system
> comes as a late acquisition laid over conceptions
> of self and of other Negroes derived from intimate,

---

[1]Stamp, Kenneth. The Peculiar Institution: Slavery
in the Ante-Bellum South (New York: Vintage Press, 1956).

and to the child often traumatic, experience within the ghetto community.

. . . The child has little opportunity to develop a more realistic image of himself and other Negroes as being damaged by whites and not by themselves.

. . . To those living in the heart of a ghetto, black comes to mean not just "stay back," but also membership in a community of persons who think poorly of each other, who attack and manipulate each other, who give each other small comfort in a desperate world. Black comes to stand for a sense of identity as no better than these distributive others. The individual feels that he must embrace an unattractive self in order to function at all.[1]

In a further discussion of a generalized black personality, Kardiner and Ovesey present a schematic illustration (Fig. 1) which suggests a cause-and-effect relationship between the historic black condition of oppression and low self-esteem.[2]

---

[1]Lee Rainwater, "Crucible of Identity: The Negro Lower-Class Family," in The Negro American, Talcott Parsons and Kenneth B. Clark, eds. (Boston: Beacon Press, 1966), pp. 160-204.

[2]Abram Kardiner and L. Ovsey, "On the Psychodynamics of the Negro Personality," in The Self in Social Interaction, Vol. I: Classic and Contemporary Perspectives, Chad Gordon and Kenneth J. Gergen, eds. (New York: John Wiley & Sons, Inc., 1968). See also, The Mark of Oppression by Kardiner and Ovesey.

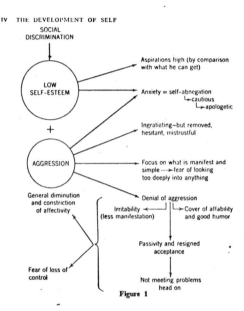

Figure 1

The theoretical orientation of Mead and Cooley along with the interpretation of black history described above have had a continuing and heavy influence on almost all black self-concept research. In Chapter III, we shall return to a discussion of some of the assumptions on which this orientation is based.

THE EMPIRICAL RESEARCH:

    I. The Early Period, 1939-1953.

        A. <u>Doll Studies:</u>

The research of Horowitz (1939), Goodman (1940), and Clark and Clark (1947) represent the vanguard of the research which established a methodology which measures the self-

concept as a single salient dimension -- race-color awareness. These studies which used dolls, puppets, and diag-
nostic play situations, presented black and white children
with a forced choice design which tested the child's awareness of race and color, the child's awareness of the adult
attitudes associated with race (color), and the child's
willingness to associate himself with a given race.

In each of these three studies, children were asked
to make choices concerning the desirability, the esthetic
beauty or the anticipated social status of colored and white
dolls and puppets. The results of all three of the studies
were consistent and indicate a preference by black and white
children for white (dolls, puppets, situations) and the
rejection of black (dolls, puppets, situations) which were
identical. The results of these pioneer studies appear to
support the conclusion that for black and white children
of northern as well as southern regions, white is good and
black is bad, or at least to some serious degree, less
desirable.

Helgerson (1943), Goodman (1946) and Seeman (1946)
also used the Doll Test, sometimes with a variation of
materials such as the use of photographs instead of dolls.
Their findings support those reported by Clark and Clark.

The Doll Test was combined with extensive interview
and observation by Radke, Tragen and Davis (1949) and Radke
and Tragen (1950). Using the forced choice situation,

these researchers gave particular attention to children's
perceptions of social roles of blacks and whites. In these
studies children were not only given the traditional Doll
Test, but they were also asked to tell stories about the
dolls and to assign them to roles, and to select one of a
series of houses (poor condition, better condition) in which
the dolls lived.

Landreth (1953) introduced an interesting variation
of the Doll Test. The children were requested to match
figures representing families of white, brown and black
color, and to insert the figures into a picture representing
a family scene.

The findings of these and other Doll Test studies of
the time were consistent: black children selected or
identified with white dolls. Also, black and white children
assigned negative rolls to black dolls.

B. Field Studies:

A number of field studies have presented an assessment of the black self-concept, although this assessment has
generally been presented in terms of a "Black personality."
Four field studies, which are especially prominent among
sociological literature about the black condition, were
conducted concurrently in different sections of the United
States. All four studies were the outgrowth of directives
by the American Youth Commission of The American Council on
Education. The findings of these studies are compatable,

and together they present a general theme of low black self-concept and a tendency toward identification with the op-pressor as a result of conflicts of caste, class and color.[1] These findings are also compatable with the previously re-ported findings of the Doll Test Studies.

The personality of eight black adolescents in the deep south was studied by Davis and Dollard (1940) who reviewed case studies of thirty-five black children between the ages of 12 and 15. .The study attempts to illustrate the effects of the economic and social restrictions imposed upon the southern black by a caste system which is based upon color, and concludes that in the deep south "for a child to come into the world with a dark skin is to have the cards stacked against him from birth." They reported a rejection of black, preference for white or "fair-skin", and an imitation of white norms and "respectability."

Frazier (1940) presented case materials for 123 boys and 145 girls interviewed in Washington, D. C. and Louisville, Kentucky. He reports "distrust and high animosity" toward high status blacks as well as whites by middle and low status blacks. However, in group color prejudice is viewed to be far less damaging in consequences than white prejudice and discrimination. The black children were generally viewed

---

[1]The fourth in this series of studies is not pre-sented by this paper because there is little specific in-formation about the self-concept in it.

to have feelings of insecurity, inferiority and low self-esteem. The study highlights the social and cultural context in which the black personality is reported to take form.

Warner (1941) presented an analysis of 805 case histories of Chicago blacks whom he classified according to "social types" based on skin color. He reported for the blacks adoption of white values for beauty. In explanation, however, he pointed out that social class and occupational status within the black community followed color stratification among men, and that color determined upward mobility through marriage for women. He implies that the preference for lighter skin damages the self-esteem of blacks.

2. The Middle Period, 1954-1963.

A. Still More Doll Tests:

Doll tests continued through this time period, although the tests were not used as frequently as during the previous period. Results continued to report low black self-concept evidenced by children's preference for white dolls.

Variations in the Doll Test during this time frame included the use of photographs, [Moreland, (1958) & (1961)]; and the use of cards depicting play situations [Stevenson and Stewart (1958)]. Subjects represented a range of geographical regions and one study in particular [Moreland (1966)] used matched samples of children from northern and southern regions. The findings reported for these studies continued to support those of the earliest time frame.

For example, Stevenson and Stewart (1958) reported low

self-concept for 93 blacks of a sample of 225 pre-school

and elementary school children of Texas. And Butts (1963)

in a study of fifty black children ages 9 to 12, reported

that the children's inaccurate perception of their own

skin color was positively related to the wish to be another

color. In his sample, the group of black children with

impaired self-esteem are reported to have perceived them-

selves less accurately in terms of skin color. The data

suggest that low self-esteem was associated with darm skin

color.

Moreland (1966) used samples of 164 black and white

children from Boston, Massachusetts and Lynchburg, Virginia,

and reported that children of both races accepted whites

as playmates. Black children in both regions tended to

prefer and to identify with members of the other race, with

southern blacks more likely to prefer whites and southern

whites more likely to reject blacks.

B. Projective Tests and Interviews:

The picture of black inferiority emerging from the

Doll Tests was supported by studies primarily conducted by

psychiatrists and psychologists who often discussed a

generalized "Negro Personality."

Kardiner and Ovesey (1951) reported from information

obtained through the psychoanalytic procedure of twenty-five blacks from among their patients. They reported that in general, blacks have low self-esteem, self-hate, in-group hostility and an inferiority complex. They gave considerable attention to black sex fantasy dreams which are interpreted to represent a desire for white identification and acceptance by whites (as the salient other). These general findings are supported by Mussen (1953) who conducted a study of the T.A.T. responses of black and white boys and reported that there were implications among the black responses of feelings of inferiority and helplessness. The black protocols were reported to reflect a general view of the environment as hostile. Few blacks were reported to have seen themselves as being respected, followed or obeyed by others, and among blacks there were more incidents of aggressive press (stress) and attitudes of indifference than among the comparative white group.

The same general findings and conclusions of Kardiner and Ovesey, and Mussen are presented by Grossack (1954) who conducted a study of 180 black subjects and reported that self-abasement was higher than for the comparable white group. However, just one year later, Grossack reported the results of a study of responses of 183 blacks to questions about what it means to be a Negro. Contrary to the above patterns, the results of this study reported race pride, ethnocentricism and positive self-esteem. Grossack reported that the subjects were found to be optimistic and to have

had an awareness of both the problems and challenges before
them.

C. Early Self-Concept Scales:

Among the earliest of the self-concept scale tests
is the study by Gordon (1963) who used the Guttman Scale to
study 315 junior college students of Los Angeles, California.[1]
Gordon reported the following rank order of the self-concepts of the groups: blacks highest, followed by Jews, non-
Jewish whites, Mexican-Americans and Orientals. The Gordon
study results present findings which are contradictory to
some of the earlier studies.

3. The Recent Time Frame, 1964-1973.

A. The Most Recent Doll Tests:

Contradictory findings among studies using the same
technique are found among the most recent Doll Tests.
Although a number of the tests of the recent time frame have
continued to report findings of low self-concept, we begin
to find studies which report different findings. Several
studies report no difference between the responses of black
and white subjects to Doll Tests. We note also that
variations in Doll Test materials were introduced during this
time frame.

---

[1]
    Reference is made here to the Guttman Social Dis-
tance Scale. See: Blalock, Hubert M. and Ann B. Blalock.
Methodology in Social Research. New York, McGraw-Hill Co.,
1968, pp. 98-103.

The previous findings of the studies which reported
low self-concept are supported by the findings of Moreland
(1965) who, varying the Doll Test through the use of photographs of black and white children, studied two pre-school
age groups of children of a southern segregated and a northern
integrated situation. Moreland reported that the black
children in both regions preferred and identified with the
white race. For Blacks self-abasement and low self-esteem
was reported; however, there was lower self-esteem among
the southern group. The findings of Moreland are compatible
with the findings of Asher and Allen (1969) who used puppets
of brown and white representation in a variation of the
Doll Test. They reported that for 341 black and white
children from Newark, New Jersey, "remarkable consistency"
between black and white preference for the white puppet
and rejection of the brown puppet. The researchers concluded
that for the black child, the rejection of the brown puppet
suggests self-abnegation.

Contrary to the previous findings, Gregor and
McPherson (1964) using a variation of the Doll Test in their
study of 83 white and 92 black children of a deep southern
metropolitan area, found "no difference" in self-esteem.
Both groups of children are reported to have had a "viable
and secure self-system." Larson and associates (1966) also
used a variation of the Doll Test and reported positive results
in a study of black and white children of a metropolitan
area. They reported that although the black children more

often incorrectly identified themselves racially than white children, they showed no significant preference (among dolls) for either race in their positive and negative role assignments.

Another of the most recent Doll Test studies which presents findings contrary to those of the earlier studies was conducted by Hraba and Grant (1970). These researchers interpreted their data as indicating that the children (89 black and 71 white children, ages 4 to 8) intended to express a liking for dolls of both races. The doll choice results were considered to reflect the children's positive interracial attitudes since they were observed to have interracial friendships. The authors also speculated that the results indicated black pride among the black children, but not an accompanying rejection of whites. It is important to note, however, that throughout the recent time frame, low self-concept continues to be reported frequently among Doll Test studies.

Although we have pointed out some variations in the Doll Test, such as the use of photographs by Moreland, and the use of puppets by Asher and Allen, by far one of the most interesting variations of the test is that of Greenwald and Oppenheim, who included a mulatto doll among the traditional choices of a dark brown and white doll. The presence of the mulatto doll was interpreted by the researchers to have offered the children a wider range of

color options. The researchers reported that although both
black and white children rejected the colored dolls, a
smaller number of black children (compared to the Clark
students) misidentified themselves. Also they reported that
the black children did not show an "unusual" tendency to
misidentify themselves although the black skin color was
unpopular. They reported that "a number" of the white
children also selected the mulatto doll, a response which
was viewed to reflect a value in offering a wider range of
color choices in the Doll Test.

One of the most recent Doll Tests has been conducted
by J. Kenneth Moreland (1972) who used this methodology
in 4 different studies since the late 1950's. Over the
years, the Moreland findings have consistently shown white
dolls to be preferred; however, in his most recent study
for one measure--self-identify--the black children in
the Kindergarten to 3rd grade did not differ significantly
in preferences from the white children. Moreland reported
findings for the study by age groups, and has stated that the
"Black is Beautiful" philosophy is not reaching pre-school
black children since at this age group compared to whites
black children have lower self-acceptance.

B. Projective Tests and Psychoanalytic Studies:
Several psychoanalytic studies may be found among
the research of the recent period. The composite of the
"Black Personality" based upon the data of these studies

continues to support the findings of the psychiatric studies
nature during the earlier periods. (See Kardner and Ovesey
and Mussen). In a very popular work, Grier and Cobb (1967)
reported the results of psychiatric analysis of selected
case studies of blacks to be: self-hate, in-group hate,
misdirected aggression, low self-esteem and feelings of
inadequacy. At the same time, Coles (1967) reported low
self-esteem and self-abnegation and negative associations
with race (color) for children who through their drawing
(incomplete drawings for blacks and smaller black figures
with respect to white figures) reflected low self-esteem
and general feelings of inferiority. The Coles data were
collected after extensive interview, observation and par-
ticipation in the play activities of black children under
stress resulting from white opposition to school desegregation.

The findings of Grier and Cobb are supported by
Hauser (1971) who conducted a longitudinal study of eleven
black, eleven white and one Puerto Rican high school students
over their four-year period of study. These students were
compared to two white matched samples. Using a specially
designed Q-sort and observation as well as frequent extensive interviews, Hauser reported results which indicate
generally among blacks "identity foreclosure" and an
absence of heroes.

C. Self-Concept Scales:

Currently, self-concept scales are by far the most
widely used methodology. They have been designed either to
measure single specific dimensions or several dimensions which
are perceived to be of some weighted value in the formation of
the self-concept. The diversity of studies using self-
concept scales is overwhelming; we note for example, that
recent studies have used larger samples (often drawing data
from cross-regional census information); and have focused
upon adult populations. Also, longitudinal studies are for
the first time available. For the purposes of discussion
here, the vast body of studies using self-concept scales
has been grouped according to age categories of the respondents.

1. Studies of Elementary and Secondary School
    Children.

The academic self-concept has been the particular
dimension of interest to several investigators. Viewing
the academic self-concept as one of the many aspects of self,
Epps (1969) and a team of researchers surveyed 377 black and
white males and 431 black and white females attending inner
city schools in a large northern and a comparable large
southern city. Using two measures of "positive" self-perception (an ability scale and a general self-esteem scale);
three measures of "negative" self-perception (a shortened
version of a test anxiety questionnaire) to measure fear of
failure; a 13-item "awareness of limited opportunities

scale;" and a 7-point scale to measure expected level of future education, Epps reported that: (1) self-esteem was significantly related to the vocabulary scores of male students but not female students; (2) there was a higher correlation between self-concept of ability and grades for northern students than for southern students; (3) self-concept of ability and self-esteem are negatively related to perception of limited opportunities, test anxiety and conformity, for both sexes. Ability and self-esteem were reported to be positively correlated with grade point average; and amount of expected education was strongly related to vocabulary score in all four samples.

The well known Coleman report also gave attention to the academic self-concept. Coleman and his associates studied 5,999,000 third, sixth, ninth and twelfth grade students in schools throughout the United States. To measure the students' academic self-concept, the students were asked:

(1) How bright do you think you are in comparison with the other students in your grade?

(2) Agree or disagree: I sometimes feel that I just can't learn.

(3) Agree or disagree: I would do better in school-work if teachers didn't go so fast.

Coleman reports that the responses to these questions "do not indicate differences between Negroes and whites . . . though there are variations among regions."

The general personality and global self-esteem of
children and youth was cf interest to two well known psychologists. Baughman (1968) conducted an extensive study of
factors effecting the general personality of black and white
children. He reports positive views of self and others of
eighth grade boys and girls of a rural North Carolina community. However, results from the M. M. P. I. administered to
some of the same subjects showed black boys slightly higher
than whites on the scale measuring "sensitivity, self-
effaciveness and suspiciousness." Black boys and girls were
reported to exceed whites on the scale measuring self-doubts,
alienation from others and convictions of being inferior to
others. These conflicting findings reported by Baughman
are especially interesting in view of the findings of
Wendland (1967) who studied a sample drawn from the same
North Carolina community. Wendland reported that the mean
self-concept score from the black sample "significantly"
exceeded that of the white students. The researcher used the
Tennessee Self-Concept Scale for the evaluation of the self-
concept of 685 black and white eighth graders from areas of
North Carolina representing the country, the village, the
town and the city on a scale from rural to urban. No evidence of self-devaluation among blacks was reported regardless of the area (urban vs non-urban).

Chad Gordon (1969) used his own self-esteem scale to
evaluate the global self-esteem of a 5% nationwide sub-
sample of 9th graders drawn from the Coleman Report Data for

1,684 students. Gordon reported that whites had "somewhat higher" self-esteem. On the other hand "somewhat higher" self-esteem for blacks compared to whites is reported by Hunt and Hardt (1969) who studied a sub-sample of 1,622 participants in the Upward Bound Programs.

Contrasted to the above findings of self-doubts reported by Baughman, "somewhat lower" black self-esteem compared to whites reported by Gordon and the "somewhat higher" self-esteem of blacks compared to whites reported by Hunt and Hardt, Bachman (1970) reports "substantially higher" self-conepts for black males compared to whites in a study of a national cross-section sample of 2,213 10th grade boys in 87 public high schools in the U. S. The Bachman findings are supported by those of Powell and Fuller (1970) who also report "significantly higher" self-concepts for blacks than whites in a study of 619 white and black pupils, grades 7-9 in urban segregated and desegregated schools in a central south region. In the next Chapter, we shall take a closer look at some factors which are associated with the irregularity of the findings of these and other studies using self-concept scales.

2. High School and College Age Students

The academic self-concept has also been studied for high school and college age students. McDill (1966) studied the academic self-concepts of 327 black students matched with whites in 15 schools. He reported that the black students had higher academic self-concepts. Emphasizing the positive value of higher education for disadvantaged students, Bartee (1967) reported an increase in the self-esteem of a sample of students in freshman to senior years of college. Using the Osgood Semantic Differential to measure academic self-concept on a cluster sample of 142 Negro and 100 white students of high school and college age in predominantly segregated schools of a deep south region, Hodgkins and Stakenas report that there is higher self-assurance and a higher score for self-adjustment for the Negro sample as compared to whites.

Within this age group, a number of studies have proposed to measure a general black self-concept. Popular among these studies are the Coopersmith Self-Esteem Scale and The Tennessee Self-Concept Scale.

The Bridgette study (1968) reported the mean self-esteem for blacks to be slightly lower than for whites for 225 high school students under 17 years of age. The Bridgette constructs included the Coopersmith Self-Esteem Scale, an 8-item defensiveness measure, a family inventory statement and the Otis Quick Scoring Mental Ability Test. However, Hodgkins and Stakenas (1968) reported positive self-concept for blacks with no difference between the levels of self-concepts for blacks and whites when SES is controlled.

Still further contradictions appear with the findings of McDonald and Gynther (1965) who were concerned with dimensions of the self-concept and used an adjective inter-

personal check list to determine the self-ideal/self-dis-
crepancy score of 261 black and 211 white high school
seniors in three schools in a southern urban community. The
data showed that blacks had "significantly higher" self-
concepts than whites.

In an evaluation of racial attitudes of 6th, 8th,
10th and 12th grade students, Moreland (1972) used the
Osgood Semantic Differential list of evaluative adjectives
and the Bogardus social distance test for ranking of ethnic
and self groups. He reported that white respondents in every
age group consistently scored their own racial category.
However, as the age of the black respondent increased from
12 to 18, they tended to evaluate black more favorably and
white less favorably and to move to no social distance with
"Black American" and to rate "White American" below all
other race-ethnic groups. Both groups of respondents are
reported to have associated "American" with "White American."

Within this age group as was the case with the
previous age group, there are conflicting reports about the
black self-concept in general and the self-concept of blacks
compared to whites.

3. The Non-School Adult Population

As previously mentioned, several of the recent studies
using self-concept scales have focused upon an adult working
population. The findings for these studies are as conflicting as the findings previously reported for the other age
groups. For example, Kohn and Schloser (1969) factor

analyzed scores on self-depreciation and self-confidence of
a nationwide sample of 3,101 adult working men. They reported that blacks were slightly ("not significantly") more self-
deprecatory but significantly more self-confident (when
controls were made for social class). On the other hand,
Crain and Weisman (1972) who used a 1-item self-esteem
scale as well as the interview to survey 1,651 blacks, ages
21 to 45 in metropolitan areas of the north (selected from
a sample of 297 city blocks in 25 different areas) reported
that northern-born blacks score as high as whites on measures
of self-esteem, Heiss and Owens (1972) conducted a data
analysis responses of a block quote sample of 1,651 blacks,
ages 21 to 41, and a matched white group to questions concerning the four traits: (1) self as an offspring, parent,
spouse, conversationalist and attractiveness to the opposite
sex; (2) athletic ability perceptions; (3) reported willingness to work; and (4) perceptions of intelligence. They
reported no difference between responses of blacks and whites
for the four traits involved. Yancey, (1972) et al., reported that for 1,179 black and white subjects living in
Nashville, Tennessee, and Philadelphia, Pennsylvania, there
is no evidence of negative effects among blacks because of
race. In the south, it is reported that blacks have higher
self-esteem and lower rates of symptoms of stress than
whites. Yancey and his associates measured self-esteem and
psychological symptoms of stress through the use of a
questionnaire survey and interviews. They employed the

22-item Langer scale of psychomatic symptoms of stress and
the Rosenberg 1965 Self-Esteem Scale.

CONCLUSION

This Chapter has presented a review of black self-
concept research over approximately 35 years. We have ar-
gued that the social psychology of Cooley and Mead in con-
junction with a recognition of the historical condition of
Black Americans, particularly of the legal-moral order of
slavery and the accompanying identification of blacks as
"something less than human," has been the foundation of a
conventional wisdom which presumed black self-derogation.

The earliest empirical research assumed self-concept
was reflected by awareness of race-color differences. Research methodology changed over time with a movement away
from this simplistic single dimension evaluation of the self
to the use of multidimensional self-concept scales. Studies
have expanded the number of respondents and have drawn from
large cross-regional samples. These more thorough studies
have provided conflicting conclusions about the black self-
concept. The black derogation hypothesis no longer so simply
explains the data. In our closer look at the research in the
next chapters, we shall, therefore, attempt to assess more
rigorously these findings to see if such an analysis highlights patterns which help us understand this broad body of
research. This Chapter concludes with a chronology of the
empirical studies 1939-1973. This table is currently the
most comprehensive review available which embraces the
total time period.

THE SELF-CONCEPT OF BLACK AMERICANS: A CHRONOLOGY BY TIME FRAMES OF EMPIRICAL STUDIES 1939-1953

Date	Author	Sample	Methodology	Results & Conclusions
				1939-1953
1939	Horowitz, Ruth E.	24 Children in public WPA nursery school, 2-5 yrs. age, 21 answers of the 24 were tabulated.	Choice Test Series: child views page bearing 2 or more pictures and is asked "show me which one is you." which one is (name of child). "Portrait Series: 10 portrait pictures shown, one at a time. Child is asked "is this you. Is this (name)."	32% of Negro boys made consistently correct identifications, 20% split out of white boys made correct consistent identifications. (No split out for girls) Identification as Negro as a factor of difference or awareness of one's own skin identified in both skin pictures or similarity. Negro boys _given a forced choice_ _devoid of this_ _given a forced choice_. Suggests "motor activity" on the part of the Negro children who identified with white.
1939	Clark, Kenneth B. and Mamie K. Clark	150 Black children from 5 W.P.A. Nursery Schools in D.C.	Modification of the Horowitz picture test. Forced choice between photographs of black and white boy to determine racial identification.	3 & 4 year olds indicate greatest amount of self-consciousness and racial identification. There were more choices of colored boy than of white boy with ... ation of choices of colored to white increasing with age in favor of colored boy. Results suggest four years old as the age of awareness of self as a distinct person as distinct from other groups of things or individuals." Assumes that choices and social identification are indicative of that "race consciousness" ... particularized self consciousness" by obvious physical characteristics.
1940	Clark & Clark	Subjects same as above.	Methodology same as above except that subjects were grouped on the basis of skin color: light, medium, dark. Only choices of white or colored boy could be made (excluded irrelevant choices of animals included in previous test).	"Consistent increase (approaching statistical significance) in choices of colored boy from the light to medium group, but probable increase from the medium to the dark group. From light to dark group statistically significant increase in choices of colored boy. Data does not support "skinful activity" theses of Horowitz, but rather than 'what one is not.' Concludes that skin color is an important factor in the 'genesis of consciousness of self and racial identification."

Date	Author	Sample	Methodology	Results & Conclusions
1940	Davis, A. and J. Dollard	Field study in the "Deep South"	Personality study of eight Negro adolescents in the Deep South. Cases were selected from thirty-five life histories of Negro children between the ages of twelve and sixteen who live in New Orleans, L.A. and Natchez, Miss.	Illustrates effects of the economic and social restrictions which impose a caste system upon the Negro of all classes and colors. Points to variations of problem among color and class groups. Children except same punishments and rewards their parents have received. Children experience caste, class, culture conflict. Concludes that in New Orleans of Natchez "to a child to come into the world with a dark skin is to have the cards stacked against him from birth." Finds rejection of black by Negroes; preference for white or "fair-skinned", imitations of white norms and "respectability".
1940	Frazier, E.F.	Field study	Case materials for 123 boys and 145 girls interviewed in Washington, D.C. and Louisville, Kyn.	Illustrates "distrust and high animosity" toward high status Negroes as well as whites by middle and low status Negroes. However in group color prejudice is viewed to be far less damaging in consequences than white prejudice and discrimination. Low self-esteem reported by observations of various factors. Generally follows the social interactionist theory of personality development (a focus upon the social and cultural context in which the personality takes form.) Negro children were generally viewed to have feelings of insecurity and inferiority.
1941	Warner, W.L. et al.	Field Study	Analysis of 805 Case histories of Chicago Negroes, Individuals in the sample were classified according to ten criteria and assigned to a "social type representing the specific combination." Test hypothesis were: (1) "...systematic subordination of Negroes to white people...has a definite effect upon the development of Negro personality. (2) Evaluations of color and other physical traits made by Negroes themselves on their own group influence the development of personality (3) Social-class position and occupational status in the Negro society here effects upon Negro personality formation."	Observes preferences for white or light-skin and white norms for beauty. Social class and occupational status follows color stratification among men and determines "upward" mobility through marriage for women. Concludes that the Chicago society is organized on a caste like basis with physical appearance having an exaggerated importance. Being a Negro has varying meanings by skin color for men and women. Generally highlights overall factors of low self esteem highlighted by preference for white or light skin color and the accompanying "respectability" and s.e.s. factors.

Date	Author	Sample	Methodology	Results & Conclusions
1943	Helgerson, Evelyn.	Variation of Horowitz and Clark technique using photographs vary-ing in race, sex and facial expres-sion.	Total of 168 subjects from Minneapolis, Minnesota. Age range, 2½-6 years.	Tendency of both colored (57.8%) and white (70.6%) to choose white child more than half the time. Among colored children there was a "decided ten-dency" to choose the colored playmate less frequently.
1946	Goodman, Mary E.	27 children (15 Negro and 12 white) age 2-9 from Ruggles Street Nursery, Boston, Mass.	Variation of Horowitz and Clark test using a diagnostic play sit-uation. Choices between black and white pictures and dolls.	Uneasiness, tension and evasion observed among Negro children but not among whites during self-identification test. Negroes tended to prefer white dolls and to reject dark dolls. Suggests inaccuracy of Negro identification reflects "not simple ignorance of self but unwillingness or psychological inability to identify with the brown doll because the child wants to look like the white doll". Rejection by Negroes of brown dolls reflect socio-cultural patterns relevant to the need and American white ideals for personal appearance. Children reflect awareness of race dif-ferences and their implications. Psychological insecurity and uncertain status of adult Negroes viewed to be reflected by the children. Negro children preferred white doll; rejected black doll; rejected identifica-tion of themselves with black doll. Self-identification self-depreciation.
1946	Seeman, Melvin	Total of 81 Negro children 3-6th grades in Ohio. Children grouped by sex and color categories using Warner Chicago color categories.	Children made self-ratings and indicated motivation for friendship choice and a "three wishes" test designed to bring out relative desirability of skin color.	Observes an "almost complete absence of skin color as a verbalized motivation" for friendship preference. Observes range of preferences for lighter skin color and "better hair" in groups of children by their skin color. Darker group prefers light skin and "good hair". Light group shows little such desire but desire to be "smarter & stronger." Data viewed to "reveal clearly their (group as a whole) commitment to the superior value of light skin." Skin color was also viewed to be associated with differences in friendships and reputation.
1947	Clark & Clark	253 Negro children ages 3-7. 134 from southern segregated schools. 119 in northern group from racially mixed schools.	Use of black and white dolls for identification by color and "desirability." Example question: Give me the doll you want to play with; give me the doll that looks bad; give me the doll that is a nice color.	Self-negation, self-depreciation, based on preference for white dolls. Confirmed that children can correctly identify racial differences. White children make more correct racial self-identifications. Black children reject adult self-identifications. Preferred white to colored; make correct racial self-identifications, but were often unable to accept the meaning of blackness in American life.

-30-

Date	Author	Sample	Methodology	Results & Conclusions
1949	Radke, Trager & Davis.	250 children, 5-6 years of age, in the K-2nd grades from six public school districts in Philadelphia, Pa. Selection of the schools was made by school administrators on the basis of various religious, ethnic and racial group representation. Breakdown of test group in: 155 white, 35 of whom are Jewish and 58 Catholic and 61 Protestant and one of undetermined religion. 95 Negro protestant children. All 250 families were mainly of lower-middle income levels with some few of low income groups.	Variations of Horowitz Clark Choice Test using a series of pictures (Social Episode Test) to study attitudes concerning racio-ethnic groups. Children were asked to project about pictures showing various scenes. Pictures were 2 black and white children in various scenes. Requests were made, such as: 'Tell me about this picture.' 'What is happening in this picture.' 'Tell me about this little boy.' For "Race Barrier" test children presented interpretations of play situations which presented opportunity for identification by race.	Negro children viewed as anxious to avoid the subject of race, which "then is painful." Negro children showed discomfort when "colored" or "white" was mentioned by tester. In telling why Negro or white does or does not want to be Negro or white, Negro children persist in meaningless or irrelevant responses" which indicate "inhibition, conflict or discomfort created by the questions." Negroes viewed to be defensive or aggressive against the white. Negro answers to questions about acceptance viewed to reflect: "child's world of experiences... his wishes; or...a defensive denial of the world he knows." A "wish expression" for acceptance is most often reflected by Negroes. Major problems of being Negro for Negro children are: social disadvantage (not being liked by people, not being asked to play, not being allowed to play)—20% of responses; children are viewed to have "learned well and accepted many of the cultural conflicts and values regarding Negro and white."
1950	Radke & Trager	242 children in kindergarten, 1st, 2nd grades in 6 Phila. public schools: 90 Negro and 152 white from middle and lower SES levels, most lower-middle and upper-lower. One school and neighborhood all white; 3 predominantly white, 5-10% black, 5th and 6th 50-95% black (one school 100% black).	Child's perceptions of social roles of Negro and white adults and his evaluations of members of each race investigated using doll materials and interview. Choice situations involving Negro and white dolls and story-telling about dolls—stories structured by E to involve social roles or circumstances of persons represented by dolls.	38% of whites introduces interpretations in which stereotypes and inferior social roles were ascribed to blacks. 10% of blacks ascribe inferior roles to blacks—mainly in relation to money and housing. % for blacks not presumed to indicate the number who are aware of social differences; not expected that blacks would express the stereotypes as freely as whites, since stereotypes involving status tends to be disparaging to blacks. Black and white tended to dress-up doll of their own race. When describing what dolls might be doing, 14% of whites gave black doll specific low status roles and 24% gave work to black doll and leisure activities to white doll. 37% reversed work and leisure roles (work to white, leisure to black). No. specific socially advantaged roles described for white doll by blacks. Both races give poor house to black doll and good house to white doll. White doll preferred to black doll and feelings of prejudice against blacks. Black choose black doll as one they like best 57%. Blacks preferring white doll mention factors of appearance or circumstance which express undervaluing of own race.

Date	Author	Sample	Methodology	Results & Conclusions
1960	Radke, Sutherland & Rosenberg	Black and white children, ages 7-13 of entire school grades 2-8; 1,475 black, SES white. School: low SES area of Pittsburgh. SES area of Pittsburgh; 75% of population is Black.	Picture test: 32 photos of black and white children (8 black boys 8 black girls, 8 white boys, 8 white girls) projected on screen on slides of 8 pictures each. 12 common stereotypes of blacks selected such as lazy, dull, dishonest, etc. and descriptions based on these stereotypes used in the tests. Each typed used in the tests. Each description was paired with an opposite characteristic: "One of these children always comes to school dirty." Picture Sociometric test: Use of same photos as Picture Test. Ss asked which child in pictures he would most like to have for a friend, second and third choices, and then asked to select 3 he would not like to have as friends. Sociometric data on child's reallife acquaintance obtained a week before giving the two tests. Child recognized on prepared form the names of children desired as friends and 3 rejected. He indicated whether the child belonged to his class in school, different grade, or lived in community but did not go to same school.	Fact that blacks assign undesirable characteristics to black pictures (when whites assign almost to undesirable characteristics to white pictures) suggests ambivalence for Blacks toward own race. 6th graders: black positive attitude toward own race perhaps reflects rebellion against acceptance of derogatory stereotypes of blacks. Increase in choice of friends, acceptance of derogatory stereotypes of blacks. Choices of of younger and older children select both black and white pictures. blacks close to half and half distribution by both black and white. (42% and 5% of black pictures chosen by younger and older children. Slightly more than half the rejections by both black and whites are of black pictures. Percentages of black pictures in all but 6th graders; 6% friendship responses consistent to point of atypical responses than percentages of choices and 40% rejection responses given to black pictures. Data conform to past tests. Whites in all situations and all ages (7-13) of 6th grade blacks on both tests. Whites who indicate more acceptance of own race than do younger blacks on both tests. Whites and blacks as friends are on attract of wish 'level express strong preference for own racial group; particularly true when choices between blacks and whites. Blacks on assignment of behavior characteristics (Picture Sociometric Test). Blacks on assignment of behavior characteristics to their own race and to whites show much less positive attitude toward own race than is chosen by whites toward white race. Like whites, blacks show tendency to assign undesirable characteristics to blacks. What results to be self-rejection and ambivalence toward own race appears again in black responses are of own race. Choices within black race on wish half of rejections are of own race. Choices within black race on wish level much lower in classroom and community—64% to 100% of choices are of blacks. Attractions and repulsions of both blacks and whites on questions of friendship related to their perceptions of personality characteristics of each race. These perceptions in which undesirable characteristics are ascribed to blacks and desirable to whites are consistent with wish of both blacks and whites to have whites as friends. Negative self-concept of minority members which plays important role in dynamics of adult minority-majority group conflicts is thus demonstrated to have beginnings in childhood.
1951	Kardiner & Ovesey	25 blacks of different ages, sex range of lower middle and upper SES.	Negro Personality Studies. Psychoanalytic Interview Techniques. Rorschach Test and T.A.T.	Low self-esteem. Self-hate. Ing-up hostility. Unrealistic concepts of ability and goals. Devalued self. Inferiority complex. Race-sex fantasies. "Mark of Oppression Personality."

-32-

Date	Author	Sample	Methodology	Results & Conclusions
1952	Boyd, George Felix	50 students; 25 black, 25 white from Portland, Oregon elementary school. Matched for IQ & SES.	Otis Quick-Scoring IQ Test. Two tests and a questionnaire administered as to determine level of aspiration.	Negro group had higher level of aspiration. Negro group higher on stated hopes and ambitions (occupational ambitions, desired material gains). Blacks more than whites expected to be above average in high school. Lower SES group had the higher level of aspirations. Suggests findings could be results of feelings of insecurity because of low status-- strong desire to improve one's conditions. Black may be prone to set goals very high because he is prepared (has better defense mechanism against defeat and disappointment) to adjust should he fail. Large amount of "race pride" among Negroes (24 of 28 people selected as greatest person in the world and person to be like were Negroes).
1952	Goodman, M.E.	104 nursery school children in four groups. 57 black and 46 white. Northern city.	Non-participant observation, participant observation, interview & variation of Clark Doll Test, using pictures and dolls, jigsaw puzzle and doll house.	Race awareness among children is by features and color. Children speak of "we" and "they". Direction of Negro children viewed to reflect: self-doubt; self-conscious concern; preference for white.
1952	Trager & Yarrow	250 pre-school and elementary age children, 5-8 years old from Pennsylvania. (155 white and 95 black).	Variation of Clark Doll Test.	Rejection of black, preference for white.
1953	Landreth, C. and D. Johnson	296 pre-school and elementary age children from California. (96 black and 192 white).	Variation of Clark Doll Test using a picture inset series with figures of white, brown and black skin color. Children asked to insert mother or child into picture (by color) and to identify themselves.	Black children showed preference of white over black, white over brown and brown over black skin color.
953	Mussen, Paul H.	50 Negro and 50 white boys at social agency summer camp. All boys from New York City, ages 9-14. Matched SES.	T.A.T. responses of Negro and white boys. 13 T.A.T. cards administered and protocols provided data.	Negroes see general environment as more hostile than whites; few saw themselves as being respected, followed or obeyed by others; more incidents of aggressive press, attitude of indifference. Implications were feelings of inferiority and helplessness.

1954-1963

Date	Author	Sample	Methodology	Results & Conclusions
1954	Grossack, M.	183 Negro respondents; 57 children ages 10-16 (individual interviews), 126 college students (open-end questions).	Ss asked: What does being a Negro mean to you? What are some of the good things about being a Negro? What are some of the bad things about being a Negro? What does the future hold for the Negro people?	Q.1--Gratifications and deprivations with the latter "generally perceived as decreasing." Pride in belonging, admiration of group talent, leaders & physical features & the attractiveness of other members. Pride to publics. Deprivation: segregation, discrimination & prejudice. Required to make personal sacrifice, be tolerant of frustration & to obey white authority. Small percentage disliked other group members (whites). More negative responses among the elementary and secondary students than among the college students.
1955	Grossack, M.M.	171 students (108 female and 63 male Negroes), and comparable white group.	Edwards Personal Preference Schedule. 225 forced-choice items which measure 15 personality needs.	Self-abasement higher among Negroes and females than among whites and males. (Note: positive scores on other needs).
1957	Trent, Richard D.	202 Negro Children & youth (112 males and 90 females) ages 9-18 from three public schools of Manhattan and Brooklyn, N.Y.	Test battery included: a checklist of statements dealing with social conformity; test designed to tax the self-feelings and self-attitude finder and SES questionnaire. Attitude finder consisted of 52 items divided into two sub-scales for measuring attitudes toward white and Negroes.	The most self-recognition ability was found to be significantly more positive attitudes toward both Negroes & whites than the least self-accepting. The ambivalent self-group expressed significantly more positive attitudes toward both Negroes and whites than did the least self-accepting group. No significant differences between the most self-accepting and the ambivalent in attitudes toward Negroes and whites.
1958	Moreland, J. Kenneth	454 pre-school age children (110 Black and 344 white) from nursery school in Lynchburg, Va.	Variation of Clark Doll Test using photographs about which questions were asked.	Racial self-recognition ability was found to be significantly higher for white than for Negro children. Negro children were observed and viewed to "unconsciously" identify themselves with the dominant, privileged race. Many who replied that they were colored "did so reluctantly and with emotional strain." On racial self-recognition 99.5% of white said they were white in contrast to 52% of the Negro children who said they were "colored." 32% of Negroes and only 5% of the white misidentified by racial self-recognition.
1958	Stevenson, Harold W. & Edward C. Stewart	225 preschool and elementary age children (93 Black and 125 white).	Variation of the Doll Technique using cards depicting play situations and dolls. Students were tested at school by E of the same race as Ss.	Higher frequency of negative attitudes among the Negro Ss; greater frequency of own race rejection; lower status assignments for black children.

Date	Author	Sample	Methodology	Results & Conclusions
1960	Rohrer and Edmonson	Field study of 20 Black adults drawn from field sample of Davis and Dollard to determine attitudes and perceptions of self.	Interview and testing (Roscheck, T.A.T., Draw-A-Figure, Bellevieu).	Attitudes were generally positive and reflected optimism associated with C.R. movement of the times. Findings do not generally reflect a mark of oppression among these "eighth generation" college and non-college adults.
1961	Moreland, J.K.	407 (126 Black & 281 white) pre-school School age children in Virginia.	Variation of Clark Doll Test using pictures of Negroes and whites.	Preference of white over black. Both Negro and white subjects preferred the white children in the pictures.
1962	Haggstrom, W. C.	30 desegregated and 30 matched segregated Negro households in Detroit constitute the samples primarily studied.	A happiness self-rating scale was devised (but not completely validated) and some reasons and data put forward for the conclusion that it can serve as an estimator of self-esteem within the range of persons and situations studied.	Members of desegregated Negro households in the study do tend to have higher self-esteem than do members of matched segregated Negro households (Wilcoxon Test, one-tailed). Some support for the explanatory conclusion that the Negro community depressed the self-esteem of its members. Data (not co clusive) suggests that Negroes with low self-esteem tend most to become residentially desegregated. Members of desegregated Negro households (as compared with members of matched segregated Negro households) (1) have greater identification with their neighborhoods, (2) tend to find being an American relatively more important and their race and religion relatively more important and their race and religion relatively less important, and (3) tend to be less hostile toward white persons and Negroes and less accepting of the existing race relations pattern.
1962	McDonald, Robert L. & Malcolm D. Gynther	354 (196 female, 159 male) Negro high school seniors who graduated in 1961/1962 from an urban segregated southern high school. 263 (132 female, 131 male) white high school seniors graduating at different segregated high school in same time from different segregated high school in same community. SSS quite skewed; however a study just completed showed that	MMPIs were administered with standard instructions by school counselors during special group testing periods.	Male Negroes obtained higher scores on all scales where differences were significant. Negro males obtained higher scores on items which presumably represent a clustering of neurotic-like items. Although there are configurational similarities between MMPI profiles of Negroes and whites, differences exist in a sufficient degree to indicate that separate norms for Negroes should be developed. Separate norms should be developed for male and female Negroes.

Date	Author	Sample	Methodology	Results & Conclusions
1962	McDonald, Robert L. & Malcolm D. Gynther	cont'd, social class had no effect on XWPI scale scores. No statistical corrections for SES differences were made. Ages of Ss ranged from 16-19 and analyses revealed no mean age differences between sex or race.		
1952	Works, Ernest	Negro tenants living in partly segregated low-income housing project of 618 units divided into 2 sections by east-west thoroughfare. 2/3 of units were on north side and 1/3 on south. Negroes occupied 54% of north units and 94% of south. Former was accepted as integrated project as Negro families were widely dispersed throughout the area with no evidence of clustering. The south side though not completely segregated was accepted as the all-Negro project.	Data were gathered by interview. Of 144 interviews conducted, 35 were with integrated wives, 33 with integrated husbands, 41 with segregated husbands. 4 sets of interview items were used to collect data. Used a self-description scale consisting of 20 pairs of opposite words. Subjects were asked to describe themselves by checking space they felt most appropriately described them. Asked to describe how they thought about themselves prior to moving into the project, the pre-project self-concept, the first checklist was completed without knowledge that a second would be requested. Subjects were not permitted to use the first description as a reference for the second description. Data contradicts the hypothesis that favorableness of self-concept depends upon social status.	Data did show that Negroes in integrated housing tend to undergo more improvement in self-concept than do Negroes in segregated housing. This suggests that an improvement in the status of the Negro is associated with an improvement in the Negro's self-concept.

Date	Author	Sample	Methodology	Results & Conclusions
1953	Ezzziel, William	262 college Blacks from the South.	Edwards Personal Preference Test to determine correlates of the Negro Personality.	"The need structure differs significantly (.01 level of confidence) from the white norm group in 8 of the 15 variables yielded by the instrument." Majority of the variables were of "a type involving direct ascendance-submission" in human relationships, i.e. dominance, deference, etc. Suggests that deference is the result of "a great fear of showing a real need for aggression". Generall found a "unique syndrome of conflicting needs"..."consistent with the findings of Dollard (1937), Kardiner and Ovesey (1951)". Caste sanctions are viewed to make a difference in Negro need patterns (by s.e.s. group).
1963	Brody, Eugene B.	19 Negro boys attending the clinics associated with the Psychiatric Institute of the University of Maryland.	Interviews and Observations. Variation of Doll Technique using hand puppets dressed in business suits.	12 of 19 boys indicated color-conflict; rejected black puppet as "bad" "not good" "sad". 7 evidenced no color-conflict. "Only 6 (about 1/3 of the boys) saw themselves and all members of their families as more closely resembling the Negroes than the white puppet and of these 6, 2 expressed some uncertainty; leaving only four of 19 boys who identified themselves and both parents as unequivocally Negro.
1963	Butts, Hugh F.	50 Negro children, ages 9-12, of the Hillcrest Center for Children, Bedford Hills, N.Y. (dependent and neglected child care institute).	Self-esteem measured by testing with California Test of Personality, Elementary Series, 153 Revision. Subset—"Sense of Personal Worth." Rating scale to measure self-esteem was utilized by social workers and counselors. Clark & Clark test used to determine perception of skin color.	Inaccurate perception of own skin color was positively related to the wish to be another color. Group of Negro children with impaired self-esteem perceived themselves less accurately in terms of skin color. Low self-esteem is associated with dark skin color.
1963	Gordon, C.	315 junior college students, Los Angeles, California.	10-item Gutman Scale	Negroes highest, followed by ... white, Mexican-Americans, Orientals on self-esteem scale.

-37-

Date	Author	Sample	Methodology	Results & Conclusions
1963	Keller, Suzanne.	46 1st and 5th grade children (Negro and white) living and attending school in "the poorer sections of New York City."	Interviews and questionnaires. Self-Concept and motivation Test containing ten incomplete sentences relating to "some wish, judgment or evaluation of the child".	Unfavorable references increased from 55 % to 65% from 1st to 5th grade. These children as a group expressed low self-esteem. Negro children "definitely" exhibit more negative self-evaluations than do white children (80% Negro & 30% white draw unfavorable self-other comparisons).
1964	Gregor, A. J. & A. Mc-Pierson	83 white, 92 Negro children (pre-school & in-school blacks) of a deep south metropolitan area.	Variation of the Clark Doll Test.	No difference. Both groups having viable and secure self-system."
1964	Marx, Gary T.	1,119 Negro adults in metropolitan areas outside the South.	Psychological Contest of Militancy. Interviews. 8-item Militancy test. 2-question Index of self-image.	10% of those with unfavorable self-image score as non-militant; 39% of those with favorable self-images were militant; 23% were neutral.
1964	Parker, S. & R. Kleiner	Psychiatric sample of 1,423 in- or out-patients of public and private agencies; sample from the Phila. Negro community, 1489. Ages 20-60; both Ss and parents born and lived in Philadelphia.	Interview and Questionnaire.	High-status Negroes have values more similar to those of white middle class; stronger desires to associate with whites; more internalization of negative attitude toward other Negroes, and weaker ethnic identification than lower status Negroes. Supports Frazier's thesis of self-hate as especially manifest among black "bourgeoisie."
1965	Bayton, James A., et al.	240 Negro students at Howard University (120 male, 120 female).	Guilford-Zimmerman Temperament Survey.	Tendency to idealize the aggressor (white) and to incorporate his negative views toward the minority group.
1965	Herman, Melvin, et al.	601 Negro Youth Corps participants, Ages 16-21 compared to samples from Catholic High school, white university, and black university in New York City.	10-item Guttman Scale (same as Rosenberg).	Harlem black youth of Youth Corps had self-esteem "little lower" than Catholic and all university youth. Brooklyn youth group had "considerably lower" self-esteem than all others.

-38-

Date	Author	Sample	Methodology	Results & Conclusions
1965	Waliver, Bruce L.	160 Negro male college students; 85Ss in 3 southern groups, 75Ss in 5 colleges throughout the country.	7-point Likert Scale composed of anti-Negro and pro-Negro items.	Theory of identification with the agressor not supported.
1965	McDonald & Gynther	216 black and 211 white high school seniors in 3 schools in a southern urban community.	Self-ideal/self-discrepancy scores based on 128 adjectives from the Interpersonal Check List.	Blacks significantly higher than whites on self-esteem.
1965	Moreland, J. K.	Pre-school age children of Lynchburg, Va. (segregated nursery schools and day-care centers). Pre-school age children of Boston, Mass. (integrated schools and play groups).	Photographs of black and white children in situations designed to measure racial acceptance; racial preference; racial self-identification and racial recognition.	Negro subjects in north and south region preferred and identified with white race. Self-abasement, low self-esteem for north and south Negro group with greater significance among southern group.
1965	Rainwater, Lee	Low-class Negro families in ghetto community.	Observation and interview, historic research.	Low self-concept; internalized view of the majority; in-group hostility; unattractive "self."
1965	Rosenberg, Morris	5,024 high school juniors and seniors from 10 public schools in New York state.	10-item Guttman Scale.	Blacks had slightly lower self-esteem than whites; 55% of whites and 61% of blacks.
1965	Coleman, et al.	Survey of 660,000 pupils.*	Control & Academic Performance of Black students. 3-item question to measure child's sense of control over his environment. *599,000 3rd, 6th, 9th, 3-item academic self-concept score. and 12th graders throughout the United States.	Negroes and other minority children show much lower sense of control of their environment than do whites. Negroes who had high self-concepts as well as high interest in school had lower sense of control compared to whites. No difference. Blacks and whites the same.

Date	Author	Sample	Methodology	Results & Conclusions
1966	Gregor & McPherson	Total of 175 (83 white and 92 black) elementary age (6-7) children.	Doll techniques.	Black children identified with black dolls. White children measured "normal" ethnocentrism. Attitude profiles were no different for both groups.
1966	Johnson, David W.	NA	A Freedom School Program of Black Studies and genoval education.	Positive effect on boys in areas of self-attitudes, equality of Negroes and whites, attitudes toward Negroes and attitudes toward civil rights. They become more confident in themselves, more convinced that Negroes and whites are equal, more positive toward Negroes and more militant toward civil rights.
1966	Larson, Richard, et al.	2 white, 7 black children in 5inner city and 2 outer city schools.	Variation of Doll Test to include role assignments for dolls.	Although black children more often incorrectly identified themselves racially than white children, they showed no significant preference for either race in their positive and negative role assignments.
1966	McDill, et al.	327 blacks matched with whites in 15 schools. Total sample of 19,000.	Academic self-concept measure.	Black children higher on self-concept measure.
1966	Meyers, Edna O.	23 good achievers (at or above grade level) and 23 poor achievers (at least two years behind in grade level) from 4th, 5th, and 6th grades of an high school in a depressed urban area (Harlem, New York).	Test battery included: s.e.s. data sheet; sentence completion test, and an Attitude Checklist. Tests Administered in home to each family member included: Family Interaction Appreciation Test, a T.A.T.	Negro boys from an economically disadvantaged environment with a positive self-concept were achievers. For all 465's, a positive self-concept correlated (.05 level) with a positive attitude towards the Negro. Negro boys who were achievers differed from underachievers in being more accepting of their ethnic identity (supported at the .01 level).

Date	Author	Sample	Methodology	Results & Conclusions
1966	Moreland, J.K.	164 (84 black, 84 white) pre-school children from Lynch-burg, Va. and Boston, Mass.	Variation of Doll Test using photographs to determine difference in self-concept between northern and southern blacks and whites of test group.	Children of both races accepted whites as playmates. Large majority in each group accepted Negro children pictured, however the % were smaller than for acceptance of whites. Negro subjects in both regions tended to prefer and to identify with members of the other race, with southern Negroes more likely to prefer whites and southern whites more likely to reject Negroes.
1966	Segal, E.	13 & 15 year old boys in eastern state boys training school.	Use of pictures in projective stimulus interview.	Lower self-concepts among Negro delinquent boys than white.
1967	Bartee, Geraldine McKerry	270 full-time students at private Negro college and a newly integrated state university. Random sample of 50 disadvantaged freshmen and 50 disadvantaged seniors from each institution. Control group of 50 white and black undisadvantaged students & 20 disadvantaged blacks from state university to determine whether any significant differences existed between disadvantaged blacks at the two institutions.	Meyers-Briggs Type Indicator as an evaluation of perception of the environment and Tennessee Self-Concept Scale as an evaluation of self-perception.	Both disadvantaged and control groups exhibited low self-concepts, with high level of contradiction within various elements of self-perception. Two of the Negro groups showed the highest self-concept scores. Findings of the study viewed to refute those of many previous researchers concerning low self-concept in blacks as compared to whites and in the disadvantaged. "The contradiction between the present study of disadvantaged college students and other studies revealing low self-concepts in young disadvantaged children, particularly Negroes, indicated that the availability of higher education to the disadvantaged, particularly Negroes, has had positive effects on their self-esteem and self-concept. The increase in self-esteem from the freshman to the senior year in college, particularly in the Negro sample, emphasized the implications of the positive value of higher education for the disadvantaged."
1967	Chetnick, Fleming & Morris	2 of 7 Black children in a southern residential treatment for 100 emotionally disturbed children.	Psychoanalytic techniques.	Rejection of black. Association of white with good and desirable as child increasingly is viewed as "normal".

Date	Author	Sample	Methodology	Results & Conclusions
1967	Coles, Robert	Not specified.	Psychiatric evaluation of children's pictures. Draw-A-Picture Technique.	Low self-esteem. Feelings of black inferiority.
1967	Forward & Williams	Subsample of 93 high school students from a 1-in-5 random sample of students from the riot area high school.	4 days of interviewing during the riot (within 5 days of the start; of the riot and before the sniping had ended). Used school data for SES and family background and attitudes. Internal-external control measured by scores on Rotter IE Scale; Rotter scale for control for individual-system blame. Coleman personal evilcency scale; Epps construct for alienation and fear of success; Rosen's Achievement value scale and Srole's Anomic Scale (selected items). Also used College Aptitude Test scores; student GPA and lists asked question about riots. 65 said good (riot justified); 21 said bad (riot was wrong); 37 respondents uncertain.	Emerging profile. Rejection of fatalistic stereotype; strong belief in ability to control events in their own lives. Realistic perception of external barriers of discrimination. Increased sense of personal efficance.
1967	Frisch, Giova A. & L. Handler	122 Negro(51 male & 71 female) and 103 white(51 male & 52 female) junior high school students. Students were from two schools located in neighborhoods which "constitute the middle to upper levels of the lower class".	Draw-A-Person Technique with drawings evaluated by independent judges to determine significant differences, if any, by Negro and white Ss.	"The hair: face area ratio was significantly greater for the drawings by the Negro children than for those by the white children. Results were viewed to show "the Negro's desire for assimilation and integration." Caution is made about the data which is based upon white normative group.

Date	Author	Sample	Methodology	Results & Conclusions
1967	Georgeoff, P.J.	Random 4th grade black and white groups from (a) same neighborhood; (b) different neighborhoods and a control group from the same neighborhood.	Black self-concept and black studies. Instruction in unit on the American Negro to selected group. Self-concept measured against control group by Piers-Harris Measure of Self-Concept.	Significant improvement in self-concepts of black children in experimental group taught unit in Negro history.
1967	Gibby & Gabler	56 black, 59 white 6th graders from 2 public schools in Atlantic City, N.J.	California Test of Mental Maturity, Elementary Short Form, and Gibby Intelligence Rating Schedule. IQ scores for Ss from school records. IRS administered to all Ss in groups of 15-25 in normal classroom setting; each S required to make judgments as to how intelligent he believed himself to be, how intelligent he believed his father, mother, teachers and friends believed him to be and how intelligent he would like to be. Data analyzed by 3 scores on IRS: (1) Reality-Discrepancy (RD) obtained by computing the difference between the converted IQ score and rating on Self Scale. (2) Self-Discrepancy score (SD) obtained by computing sum of differences between rating on self scale and the ratings on father, mother, teachers, friends scale with regard to algebraic sign. (3) Ideal-Discrepancy score obtained by computing difference between rating on self scale and rating on Wish scale.	Mean discrepancy score of blacks were larger and more positive than whites. For both blacks and whites self-concept, as measured by Reality-Discrepancy scores on self-ratings on intelligence is influenced by both sex and intelligence. For males of low IQ, whites tended to have larger IQ, blacks tended to have larger RD discrepancies. For high IQ Ss differences were not found between blacks and whites, males and females. Results generally support hypothesis that black and white children differ significantly in self-concept as measured by self-ratings on intelligence. Blacks achieved significantly greater discrepancies between their actual IQ scores and their ratings on the Self scale than whites. Relative degree of these discrepancies indicates that white children tended to see themselves more accurately and realistically, while blacks tended to overrate their intellectual abilities. For Self-Discrepancy scores, whites perceptions of themselves tended to be more congruent with their estimations of how they believed others perceived them than were the perceptions of blacks. Differences for the 2 groups in discrepancies between Self-Ratings and Wish ratings, while not significant were in the expected direction. Again whites tended to be more realistic in their aspirations than blacks.

Date	Author	Sample	Methodology	Results & Conclusions
1967	Katz, Irwin	Negro male college students.	NA	In work teams composed of Negro and white students of similar intellectual ability, Negroes are passively compliant, rate their own performance as inferior even when it's not, and express less satisfaction with the team experience than do their white companions. These results are seen as due to social threat and/or failure threat: In situation that was low in both social threat and failure threat result was better performance by blacks in presence of whites than in presence of other blacks, suggesting incentive value of success was greater in white environment. But when threat of strong electric shock was introduced, the white setting became less favorable to performance than black one. Thus vulnerability to stress was greater in white condition. Among Florida black college students, anticipated intellectual comparison with black peers was found to produce higher level of verbal performance than anticipated comparison with white peers, in accordance with assumption that subjective probability of success was lower when expected comparison was with whites. In Tenn., black undergraduates responded more favorably to white norms than to black norms when the tester was black, but showed a reverse trend when the tester was white.
1957	McMicht, Ronald	152 10th grade students from three high schools in the same city. 38 Negro and 38 whites were in integrated schools and were matched with 36 Negroes and 33 whites in segregated schools.	Semantic Differential Scale was rating instrument to determine attitudes. Scale was presented at the beginning and end of the school year. Self-concept was defined as "Myself".	In integrated school: Negro females and white males increased more in their rating of the self-concept than did white females and Negro males. In segregated school: Negro males and white females increased more in their rating of the self-concept than did Negro females and white males.
1967	Taylor, Charlotte P.	Public school pupils undergoing the first year of desegregation compared with boys and girls enrolled in segregated or already desegregated schools.	Self-Social Symbols Test of Henderson, Long and Ziller. Test was administered to sixth graders upon entrance to 7th grade (onset of desegregation) and at the close of seventh grade.	Negro and white children showed significantly different self-concepts in the dimensions of centrality, dependency, individuation and power. Differences are viewed to reflect the "differential caste positions of the two races in American society. Attendance in segregated schools viewed to "intensify" these differences for one or both races. "Negro and white children reacted differently in desegregation: Negroes tend to decrease in self-esteem following an initial rise; whites tend to increase in centrality following an initial decrement."

Date	Author	Sample	Methodology	Results & Conclusions
1967	Wylie, R.C. & E.B. Hutchins	3,422 (252 black) from northern (Pa.) secondary schools.	Self-report questionnaire to evaluate self-estimation, with a focus upon the academic self-concept.	"No support for the commonly assumed hypothesis that Negroes' expressed self-estimates are lower than whites'". The Negro self-regard was not depressed. Suggests that results might reflect "a combination of unrealistic long-range dreaming while ignoring realistically necessary steps to the future goal" with respect to Negro estimate of ability to go to college, while making below expected grade averages for college preparation.
1967	Yeatts, Pearline P.	8,793 (1/3 Negro) students, grades 3-12 in a "cosmopolitan north central" Florida public school system. Focus was also upon creating normative data which could be used in assessing the self-report (using dimensions) of self which emerged for the subjects).	Gordon's "How I See Myself" self-report scale.	Self-concept conceptions varied with age and sex. Self-report did not vary according to race and s.e.s. "Although each group was unique in regard to the dimensions of self-emerging, more common than unique factors emerged for each of the groups.
1968	Baughman, E. Earl & W. Grant Dahlstrom	136 children (78 Negro) ages 13-17.	Interview to obtain children's report on their worlds. Also used teacher ratings and peer ratings.	Blacks here positive self-concepts, are happy with themselves, popular with peers and have a happy home life. Reflect high vocational and educational aspirations and are optimistic about their realizations.
1968	Baughman, E. Earl and W. Grant Dahlstrom	8th grade boys and girls (1,222; 742 blacks & 460 white) of rural North Carolina. Ss lived under racially segregated pattern.	MMPI. 550 statements which range widely over views of one's self and others, personal feelings and social attitudes, physical and mental symptoms, beliefs, habits and past experiences.	Negro boys slightly higher on scale 6 -- "sensitive...self-effacing, suspiciousness." Negro boys and girls exceed white on scale 8, self-doubt, alienation from others, convictions of being inferior or different". "...by the time these children have reached eight grade...many of the attitudes, beliefs and self-perceptions that differentiate white and Negro adults have already appeared in the self-reports...Negro children describe themselves, and the world as they know it, in terms of estrangement and cynicism. ...yet they are not just reflecting strong and pervasive negative feelings about themselves. On scale III and V (personal faults and peccadillas) they are likely to place themselves in a moderately favorable light...on scale II, ... /they/ describe themselves as /middle-class in orientation and value/. In the area of emotional ties, /they/ show

Date	Author	Sample	Methodology	Results & Conclusions
1969	Baughman, E. Earl & K. Grant Dahlstrom			cont'd. pervasive mistrust of themselves and others, extreme pessimism, ...and expectations that people will be self-seeking, dishonest, and double-dealing. ...attitudes extend to social institutions and agencies as well."
1968	Bienvenu, Millard J.	Eighty subjects drawn from 1200 male youth from an Office of Education Study of "culturally deprived" families. Experimental group: 40 youth who transferred from Negro schools into predominately white schools in North Florida; control group: subjects who had always attended an all-Negro school and continued their enrollment in the same school.	Index of Adjustment and Values and the Taylor Manifest Anxiety Scale.	No significant difference in self-concept of the experimental group and the control group from the preintegration to the post integration situation. High self-concept was generally correlated with lower anxiety.
1968	Bridgette, R. E.	225 high school students under age 17. 39 black males, 53 black females; 78 white males, 82 white females.	Coopersmith Self-Esteem, 8-item defensiveness measure. Family inventory statement. Otis Quick Scoring Mental Ability test for IQ.	Mean self-esteem scores for blacks slightly lower than for whites.
1968	Greenwald & Oppenheim	75 nursery school children (39 Negro & 36 white) ages 4 or 5 from integrated and nonintegrated schools of N.Y. suburb.	Clark Doll Test varied to use a mulatto as well as a dark brown and white doll.	Both Negro and white children rejected the colored dolls, however, a smaller number of Negro children (compared to Clark students) misidentified themselves (30% in Clark compared to 13% for this experiment). Negro children did not show an unusual tendency to misidentify themselves although the Negro's skin color was unpopular among the Negro children.

Date	Author	Sample	Methodology	Results & Conclusions
1968	Grier & Cobbs	Selected case studies.	Psychiatric analysis.	Self-hate. In-group hate. Misdirected aggression. Low self-esteem. Feelings of inadequacy.
1968	Hodgkins, E.J. & R. Stakenas	Cluster sample of 142 Negro and 100 white Ss of high school and college are in predominantly segregated institutions. (Representative of Negro and white college and high school students of a deep south region.)	Social origin questionnaire. Osgood Semantic Differential Self-Concept Measure. (Academic Self-Concept measured.)	Positive self-concept of Negroes. No significant differences between Negro and white on self-concept when SES controlled. Higher self-assurance for Negroes. Higher self-adjustment for Negroes.
1968	Long & Henderson	144 elementary school students (72 Black & 72 white) from a rural southern community.	Instrument was the Pre-school form of the children's self Social Constructs Test (CSSCT) which measures self-esteem. White students were the control group.	Lower self-esteem for the Black (disadvantaged) group. Significantly lower self-esteem, less realistic self-concept of color, less identification with father, greater identification with mother and teacher than was the case for (white-advantaged) control group. Identification with the white viewed to support the idealization theory of Kardiner and Ovesey.
1968	McDonald, R.L.	218 Negro and 310 white high school seniors from rural segregated schools of the south.	Interpersonal check list which analyzes self and other ratings in terms of dominance and love scores.	"Negro adolescents describe themselves as more dominant (assertive, aggressive, leadership qualities) in interpersonal situations than did white adolescents." Finding viewed as "incompatible with the demands imposed on their behavior as minority group members in a continuing dominant white society."
1968	Wayne, Dennis	80 students at Howard University, 1957. 88 students at Howard University, 1967.	Analysis of drawings of human figure to note representation of Negro or white. Draw-A-Man Test.	"Over a 10-year period, the number of drawings representing Negroes has risen from zero (students, 1957) to 15% (students, 1967). The majority of the drawings (82%) still represent Caucasians. Favorable attitude toward own appearance (self) is not viewed to be reflected by drawing in the test.

-47-

Date	Author	Sample	Methodology	Results & Conclusions
1968	Wendland, M.M.	665 Negro and white 8th graders from 4 areas of North Carolina represent- ing country, village, town and city areas.	Tennessee Self-Concept Scale supplemented by 2 specially derived WPI scales and family status questionnaire.	No evidence of self-devaluation among Negroes regardless of area of dent Negroes. Trend toward more positive self-concepts among rural resi- self-concept score of N significantly exceeds that of others. Mean
1968	Williams & Byers	NA	Tennessee Self-Concept Scale.	"Pervasive" difference between Negro and white self-esteem. Negro self- esteem significantly lower than whites. Negro self-esteem in integrated schools not significantly higher than Negroes in segregated schools. Blacks low in self-confidence, defensive in self-descriptions, confused concerning identity.
1969	Asher & Allen	341 white and Negro children from Newark, N.J. area. 186 Negro and 155 white, ages 3-8.	Puppets of brown and white rep- resentation. Questions adapted from Clark & Clark, 1947.	Negro and white children rejected brown puppet. "Remarkable" consistency between Negro and white preference for the white puppet and rejection of the brown puppet. For the Negro this suggests self-abnegation.
1969	Bass, E.Jordan	88 students of 9th grade assigned to four groups of differing racial group compo- sition.	Course composed of sixteen units dealing with morals, values and cultural differences was taught in sessions 3½ hours long in two groups. Integrated group; segre- gated group of black and white groups. Bills Index of Adjustment and Values. High School Form was used to reveal reported self- concept; regard for self and others.	No significant change in concept of self or acceptance of self on the part of Negro or white students as a result of subject matter. Negro students taught in integrated seminars tend to perceive their peers as being more accepting of themselves while Negro students in segre- gated seminars tend to perceive their peers as being less accepting of themselves. Negro students taught in a segregated group and white students taught in an integrated group tended to experience a positive change in self-concept. Caucasian students taught in a segregated group and Negro students taught in an integrated group experience negative change.

Date	Author	Sample	Methodology	Results & Conclusions
1969	Caplin, Morris D.	180 children from which were selected 60 children from the intermediate grades of elementary schools in a small city in northern New Jersey matched on the basis of age, grade, sex, race, intelligence, and s.e.s. (30 white, 30 Negro).	Self-concept measured by a self-report instrument developed at the Horace-Mann School. The instrument presented fifty items which "seemed to present clear examples of self-concept definitions: self as personal/social."	Significant differences in self-concept between 90 white and 90 Negro pupils in the sample group with the Negro group self-concept lower at the .05 level of significance. Both white and Negro children attending the de facto segregated school have less positive self-concepts than do the children attending desegregated schools and there is a significant positive relationship between self-concept and academic achievement.
1969	Carpenter & Busse.	80 children (white and Black) of 1st and 5th grade of welfare mothers.	Bi-polar self-concept dimensions measured by a "Where Are You Going" Test Game.	No overall race differences in self-concept found. Negro children do not become increasingly more negative in their self-concepts from 1st to 5th grade than do white children of equivalent social status.
1969	Epps, Edgar G.	Survey of high school students attending inner-city schools in a large northern city and a large southern city. 377 Negro and white males; 421 Negro and white females.	Vocabulary tests and questionnaires administered. All data except grades are based on these self-report instruments. Measure of ability used was an expanded version (60 items) of the Miner Vocabulary Test (1957). Two measures of positive self-perception were used. The first scale is a self-concept of ability scale; a general self-esteem scale based on Rosenberg (1965); 3 measures of negative self-perception were: a shortened version of Taylor Anxiety Questionnaire used to measure fear of failure; Scale measures a passive conforming orientation toward the world. Students' perceptions of limited opportunities for success were	For both sexes, self-concept of ability and self-esteem are negatively related to perception of limited opportunities, test anxiety and conformity. SES is significantly and positively related to self-concept of ability, but the correlation coefficients are very small. The negative correlation of SES with perception of limited opportunities and conformity is slightly higher. Only one significant relationship is found between test anxiety and SES. None is found between self-esteem and SES. Self-concept of ability and self-esteem are positively correlated with grade point average. Grade point average and amount of expected education are also strongly related to vocabulary score in all 4 samples. Perceptions of limited opportunities is significantly related to vocabulary score among southern students, but is not significant for northern students. The regional difference in the effect if test anxiety is in the opposite direction. Self-esteem is significantly related to vocabulary scores of male students but is not related to the scores of female students. The correlation of self-concept of ability and grades is higher among northern students than among southern students.

Date	Author	Sample	Methodology	Results & Conclusions
1969	Epps, Edgar G.		cont'd. measured by a scale based on a 13-item "Awareness of limited opportunities scale." Students were asked how far they would like to go in school if they could go as far as they desired, and how far they actually expected to go in school. The latter item was used as a 7-point scale to measure expected level of future education. Socioeconomic status was determined by using either father's occupation as reported by students or mother's education as reported by students as single indicators of family status.	
1969	Gordon, Chad	5% nationwide subsample of 9th graders of Coleman Report Data (1,684 students).	Global Self-Esteem based on: basic self-acceptance, self-rated brightness, sensed academic acceptance, sensed general competence.	Whites "somewhat" higher self-esteem.
1969	Guggenheim, Fred	29 Negro and 27 white drawn from 162 children in seven 6th grade classes from an elementary school in Manhattan, New York. School had equal enrollment of Negro, white, Puerto Rican and Latin American pupils. High and low self-esteem were defined on a median split. The final sample (56) consisted of children of equal divisions of high and low self-esteem.	Draw-a-Person Test. Set of 10 semantic differential scales and a specifically designed achievement test.	Low self-esteem white pupils had higher expectations for achievement than low self-esteem Negro pupils, but there was no difference between high self-esteem white pupils. However, "Results indicate that the generally held assumption that Negro pupils have low self-esteem may not be a valid one...To the extent that self-esteem problems exist for these children the results...indicate that they might lie in factors other than the self-evaluative one....There is strong evidence...that many disadvantaged Negro children school problems center around low achievement and not low self-esteem."

-50-

Date	Author	Sample	Methodology	Results & Conclusions
1969	Henderson, Norman B.	398 children (232 Negro and 466 white) followed by the U. of Oregon Medical School Staff. Ages were 7 years.	Draw-A-Person Technique, Children display a self-image through drawings of human figures. Total score on the test is an indicator of the completeness of the drawing (to include complete faces, arm appendages and hands,... complete human figure).	The mean scores were derived for each group (black and white). Results partially support Coles and partially support Hammer and others - Negro children drew insignificantly more complete whole figures and significantly more complete faces; fewer and less complete hands and nonsignificantly fewer arms than the white group. "If it can be assumed that the Negro children...were projecting self-images, and, therefore, drawing Negro children, then the results contradict the observation of Coles (1964) who found that Negro children, when they draw Negroes, produce less complete faces."
1969	Hunt & Hardt	Sub-sample of 211 blacks and 90 whites from sample of 1,622 adolescents in "Upward Bound Programs."	Rosenberg self-esteem scale.	Blacks somewhat higher both before and after participating.
1969	Kohn, M.L. & Carmi Schsser	Nationwide sample of 3,101 adult working men.	Factor-analyzed scores on self-depreciation and self-confidence.	Blacks slightly (not significantly) more self-deprecatory but significantly more self-confident when social class controlled.
1969	Roth, R.W.	Groups of same SES from 2 segregated & integrated 5th grade classes in public schools in Pontiac, Mich. Experimental group given black studies. Control group not given Black studies.	Change in pride and self-concept after exposure to black studies. Semantic Differential and Osgood, Adjective List used to assess racial pride. Farrah, et al., Self-Concept & Motivation Inventory.	In general, black students do not have poor self-concepts. Students provided with black studies have positive racial pride; and significant favorable differences in self-concept over those not provided with study program.
1969	Soares & Soares	514 Subjects of metropolitan areas; 228 of disadvantaged; and 285 advantaged of grades 4-8.	Soares and Soares Self-Concept Scale. 20 bi-polar adjectives to measure self, ideal self & perceived other self.	Disadvantaged group had positive self-perceptions higher than the advantaged groups. Both groups had and self-perceptions neither "overly high nor unduly low". Disadvantaged do not have lower self-esteem or lower sense of personal worth.

Date	Author	Sample	Methodology	Results & Conclusions
1970	Bachman, J.G.	National cross-section of 2,213 10th grade boys in 87 public high schools in the U.S.	10-item Rosenberg measure of self-esteem. 3 questions of academic self-concept.	Without adjustment for s.e.s. Black males substantially higher than whites on measured self-esteem. With adjustment, the results were increased in higher scores of self-esteem for Blacks compared to whites. Without control for s.e.s., Southern Blacks had slightly lower self-concepts than whites. When controlled for s.e.s., Southern Blacks have self-concepts "relatively" higher than whites.
1970	Krebs & Grant	89 black, 71 whites, ages 4-8. 89 blacks represented 60% of the black children in kindergarten thru 2nd grade in Lincoln, Neb. public schools. Whites randomly drawn from classrooms containing black respondents.	Clark Doll Technique.	Response pattern—doll of one race to requests (1) and (2), doll of another race to request (3) manifested by 42% of blacks and 54% of whites. Response pattern—doll of one race to requests (1) and (2) manifested by 51% of blacks and 62% of whites. 4-yr. olds excluded because of small N. 8-yr-olds excluded because they still being in 2nd grade would possibly confound age comparisons. Data appear to support proposition that children change their preferences because they intend to express a liking for both races, not because of cognitive incapacity. Results suggest the use of doll technique as a measure of racial ethnocentrism is inappropriate, reasonable that children changed their racial preferences to express their friendships. Also suggestion that doll technique indicates black pride among blacks but not attendant rejection of whites.
1970	Johnson, H.E.W.	Black and white college students.	Tennessee Self-Concept Scale. Student Theme Evaluations.	Significantly higher self-concept scores for black college students than for whites. Significant correlations between total positive scores and composite theme evaluations.
1970	Powell, G. J. and M. Fuller	617 Negro and white junior high students in a city in the central south. 149 Negro students from desegregated schools, 155 Negro students from segregated schools.	Tennessee Self-concept Scale. Powell-Fuller Socio-Familial Questionnaire.	"The higher scores on the self-concept scale were attained by Negro students in segregated or predominantly Negro (80%) schools. Negro boys irregardless of the racial composition of the school, scored higher than Caucasian boys. Negro boys in desegregated schools scored higher than Negro girls in desegregated schools.

-52-

Date	Author	Sample	Methodology	Results & Conclusions
1970	White & Richmond	111 5th graders from economically advantaged predominantly white school and sample of 98 economically deprived black 5th graders in predominantly black (90%) school.	Coopersmith Self-Esteem Inventory; Osgood's Semantic Differential Adjective Test.	No difference for blacks and whites in self-concept or feelings about peers.
1970	Williams, R. L. and Harry Byars.	22 Negro students from the 11th grade attending newly desegregated schools, 31 Negroes in segregated schools with at least one white instructor, and 41 Negro pupils in segregated settings with all-Negro faculties. All schools were located in the "deep South".	The Tennessee Self Concept Scale.	"Negro students in totally segregated environs made minimal improvement on most self-concept dimensions. Negro Ss in newly desegregated schools made significantly greater advancement on physical self-esteem measures than the other groups. On total self-evaluation Negro students in segregated schools with white instructors made significantly greater pre-posttest gains than the other groups. ...In general, study demonstrates that academic integration does have a positive affect on Negro self-esteem...While the data indicate pervasive improvement in the self-concepts of Negro students, they also denote that despite those increments Negroes are still substantially below the [national] normative means on most dimensions of self-evaluation."
1971	Hauser, Stuart T.	Black and white high school boys, over a 4-year period. 2 matched samples. Sample of 11 Negro, 11 white and 1 Puerto Rican.	Observation. Specially designed Q-sort and multiple individual interview.	Generally among blacks; identity foreclosure, absence of heroes among blacks, consistent stable fantasies.
1971	Rosenberg & Simmons.	1,900 children grades, 3-12 from Baltimore, Md. schools.	Rosenberg Self-Esteem.	Blacks measured higher self-esteem than whites. At secondary level, Blacks in segregated schools had higher self-esteem than those in integrated schools.
1972	Crain & Weisman	Survey of 1,651 blacks, ages 21-45 in metro-politan areas of the north selected from sample of 297 city blocks in 25 different areas.	10-item self-esteem table. Survey and interview.	Northern-born blacks score as high as whites on self-esteem.

Date	Author	Sample	Methodology	Results & Conclusions
1972	Heiss, J. & S. Owens	Block quota sample of 1,661 blacks, ages 21-45 from northern metropolitan area; 343 whites from respondent sample of 1,526 whites, matched for same SES as black sample.	Data analysis of survey information from NORC block quota sample.	No difference between blacks and whites for the 4 traits involved: (1) self as an offspring, parent, spouse, conversationalist, and attractiveness to opposite sex; (2) athletic ability; (3) willingness to work; and (4) intelligence.
1972	Morland, J. Kenneth	153 (103 white - 50 black) kindergarten and primary grade children (k-3rd grade) from Lynchburg, Va. public schools.	For k-3rd grade: Variation of Doll Test. A picture-interview test which uses 8 x 10 pictures showing black and white children in various situations. For Older Children: Ten pairs of evaluative adjectives from Osgood's List (Osgood's Semantic Differential). Bogardus social distance test used for ranking of ethnic and self groups.	For k-3rd grade: Test evaluated racial acceptance, racial preference, racial self-identification, racial bias. Black children do not show as favorable an attitude toward theirs. Statistically significant differences: blacks were more likely to accept whites than whites to accept blacks; compared to whites, blacks were less likely to prefer their own race, to say they had rather be children of their own race, to say that children of their own race were prettier, better students, and nicer than whites. Only on one measure, self-identity, did the black children not differ significantly from the white children. Pre-school blacks were even less likely than the in-school blacks to accept members of their own race, etc. Author views this to reflect the message from American society that "it was preferable to be white than black" with pre-school situation offering little balance to this general focus. Author observes that focus upon "black is beautiful" and black heroes is not reaching pre-school black children, and is not reflected among in-school black children tested since compared to in-school whites, blacks have lower self-acceptance. Older children - 6th, 8th, 10th, & 12th grades: White respondents in every age group consistently scored their own racial category most favorably and with the least social distance. As the age of black respondents increase (from 12-18) they tend to evaluate black more favorably and white less favorably...they move to no social distance with "Black American" and to rate "White American" below all other race-ethnic groups. Both groups associated "American" with "White American".

Date	Author	Sample	Methodology	Results & Conclusions
1972	Yancey, W.L. et al.	Black and white adults living in Nashville, Tenn., & Philadelphia, Pa. Total of 1,179--602 whites and 577 blacks (questionnaire). Interview of 352 black and 350 white in Nashville, and 215 blacks and whites in Phila.	Measure of self-esteem and psychological symptoms of stress, obtained through questionnaire survey, and interview. SES information from Census. For interview: 22-item Langner scale of psychosomatic symptoms of stress and Rosenberg's Self-Esteem Scale (1965).	No evidence of negative effects among blacks because of race. In the south, blacks have higher levels of self-esteem and lower rates of reported symptoms of stress.

CHAPTER II

SOME PROBLEMS IN THE STUDY OF THE SELF-CONCEPT
OF BLACK AMERICANS

In the previous Chapter we have considered a body of empirical studies from 1939 to 1973 which propose to measure the self-concept of Black Americans. The highlights of this research have been presented in a summary table to which continued reference will be made. The purpose of this Chapter is to consider some problems in the study of the self-concept by reviewing a body of studies to see if some regular patterns emerge which support the generalization of low self-concept, or indeed to observe the extent to which any generalizations about the black self-concept can be made. The body of research as reviewed below presents conflicting results. The incidence of conflicting results is so overwhelming that there emerges an obvious problem of validity. We shall come to see how the problem of self-concept definition and the validity of the measurement instruments relate to the theoretical orientation of the various studies as well as to the interpretations of study findings.

Two major problems associated with the research will be considered: (1) the problem of a definition of self-concept. (2) The problem of the validity

of instruments for the measurement of the black self-
concept. In this Chapter we shall concentrate upon the
problem of validity, and the problem of a definition of self-
concept will be discussed in Chapter III.

THE CHOICE OF THE STUDIES:

For purposes of analysis, eighty-three studies have
been selected for which data and a discussion and interpretation of results could be obtained from a published report
of the study. It should be noted that in some instances
several published articles have presented data and discussions related to various aspects of a single study. In
these instances, each published article has been treated as
a separate study.[1]

---

[1]The eighty-three studies are: Clark & Clark (1939);
Horowitz (1939); Clark & Clark (1940); Davis & Dollard (1940);
Frazier (1940); Warner, et at. (1941); Helgerson (1943);
Goodman (1946); Seemen (1946); Clark & Clark (1947); Radke
et al. (1950); Tadke, Trager (1950); Radke, et al. (1950);
Kardiner & Ovesey (1951); Boyd (1952); Trager & Yarrow (1952);
Landreth (1953); Mussen (1953); Grossack (1954); Grossack
(1957); Moreland (1958); Stevenson & Stewart (1960); Rohrer &
Edmonson (1960); Moreland (1961); McDonald (1962); Works
(1962); Brazziel (1963); Butts (1963); Haggstrom (1962);
Gordon (1963); Keller (1963); Gregor & McPherson (1964);
Parker & Kleiner (1964); Bayton (1965); Herman et al. (1965);
Maliver (1965); McDonald & Gynther (1965); Moreland (1965);
Rainwater (1965); Rosenberg (1965); Coleman, et al. (1966);
Gregor & McPherson (1966); Larson et al. (1966); McDill (1966);
Moreland (1966); Segal (1966); Bartee (1967); Coles (1967);
Gibby & Gabler (1967); Wylie (1967); Baughman & Dahlstrom
(1968); Bridgette (1968); Greenwald & Oppenheim (1968);
Grier & Cobbs (1968); Hodkins & Stekanas (1968); Long &
Henderson (1968); McDonald (1968); Wendland (1968); Wms. &
Byers (1968); Asher & Allen (1969); Carpenter & Busse (1969);
Gitter & Satow (1969); Gordon (1969); Guggenheim (1969);
Henderson (1969); Hunt & Hardt (1969); Kohn (1969); Roth

To facilitate discussion and the presentation of data, the eighty-three studies have been divided into three time frames, the same as Chapter 1. Initially, these studies are classified as showing high or low black self-concepts. Throughout the discussion that follows the term low self-concept has been used when the researcher clearly states a finding of low self-concept as opposed to high or no difference according to some norm which the author defines. In instances where the conclusion of self-concept is not implicitly stated by the researcher, I have included in the low self-concept category all studies where the author presents conclusions such as: self-negation; ambivalence towards race; self-depreciation; identification with the oppressor; preference for a white identity over a black; a clear rejection of a black identity; or the over-whelming assignment by blacks to blacks of stereotype status and roles. It should be pointed out that in the large majority of instances the conclusions about high or low self-concept are explicit or clearly implicit, although the norm is not necessarily clear. Only in a few instances has a personal judgment been made, and in such instances the guidelines presented above have been employed.

(Continued) (1969); Soares & Soares (1969); Bachman (1970); Hraba & Grant (1970); Powell & Fuller (1970); White & Richmond (1970); Wms. & Byers (1970); Powell (1971); Rosenberg & Simmons (1971); Crain & Weisman (1972); Heiss (1972); Yancey (1972); Powell (1973).

In addition the studies were grouped into one of five technique categories established on the basis of the primary method of measurement for each study. The technique categories always appear in the data or discussion in an order #I through #V according to the category most frequently used during the initial time period.

The technique categories into which the study methodologies have been grouped for consideration here are:

I.   Forced Choice Identification --

This category includes methodological approaches which require a forced choice identification of dolls, photographs, puppets, etc., by color or race and the expression of a preference for the selected medium as well as an assignment to the selected media various roles and social status. The method involves the presentation to the subjects of the media which is duplicated identically to represent black or white. The subject is then requested to select the medium, either white or black, in response to requests such as: "Give me the doll that you like to play with -- or like best." "Give me the doll that is a nice doll" or "Give me the doll that looks bad," etc.

Variations of the request have been made, and in instances when doll families have been used requests have been made, such as: "Give me the doll

that is going to work," "Give me the doll that
lives in this house, or that lives in the big
house," etc. The responses are noted and the data
are complied to report the frequency of the subject's response to the various requests through a
choice of black or white, or in instances of variations of the technique, through the assignment
of various roles and status to the dolls because
of color or race. The open-end interview has
usually been an accompanying methodology to this
technique. The technique has become popularly
known as the "Doll Test".

II. Field Studies –

This technique category includes those methodologies which primarily comprise the case study
approach; that is, a combination of the methodologies of both participant and non-participant observation, the open-end interview and the use of
both historical research and case histories. The
descriptive studies considered in this Chapter are
studies which have made some specific statement
about the self-concept of Black Americans, and
which have a clearly defined sample as opposed to
the presentation of self-concept information which
is based upon a composite with no clearly defined
sample.

III.   Interviews -

Included in this category are those studies
which use an unscaled or informal questionnaire or
the interview for gathering data.

IV.   Projective Tests -

This category includes those studies which
have used the M.M.P.I., the T.A.T., the Q-Sort and
the Draw-A-Doll methodology popular among psychologists.

V.   Self-Concept Scales -

Included in this category are those studies
which propose: (1) to present some mean self-
concept score based upon the evaluation of several
weighted dimensions of the perceived self-concept[1],
or (2) to measure the self-concept in terms of
some score along a scale for a single dimension.[2]

Tables 1, 2 and 3 which follow are concerned with the
research techniques used by the eighty-three studies. From
tables 2 and 3 may be observed the trends in the use of the
various methodologies and the frequency of accompanying findings of low self-concept.

_____

[1]
For an example, see discussion of the Tennessee Self-
Concept Scale, Chapter I.

[2]
For an example, see discussion of the Doll Test
techniques, Chapter I.

Table 1. The Relative Frequency of Use of Five Techniques for Measuring Self-Concept for Eighty-Three Studies, 1939-1973.

Technique Category	Use of Technique as % of Total Number of Techniques							
	1939-1953		1954-1963		1964-1973		1939-1973	
I. Forced Choice Identification	(12)	67%	(5)	33%	(9)	18%	(26)	31%
II. Field Studies	(3)	17%	(1)	7%	(1)	2%	(5)	6%
III. Interviews	(2)	11%	(4)	27%	(4)	8%	(10)	12%
IV. Projective Tests	(1)	6%	(1)	7%	(4)	8%	(4)	8%
V. Self-Concept Scales	(0)	--	(4)	27%	(32)	64%	(36)	43%
Totals	N=18	100%	N=15	101%	N=50	100%	N=83	99%

As may be observed, there has been a substantial decline in the frequency of the use of Technique Categories I and II, although Technique I which has declined in frequency of use is the second most frequently used technique overall. Technique III which was used with increased frequency during the second time frame was used with decreased frequency during the most recent time frame. Technique IV was used with increasing frequency from the period of the initial time frame to the most recent time frame. Among the studies considered, Technique V came into use in the early 50's and has experienced an increased frequency of use since that time. It is currently the most frequently used technique category for the measurement of the self-concept of black Americans.

It is of interest to consider the relationship
between the use of the various techniques and the frequency
of findings of low self-concept. Table 2 reports the
frequency of the use of the technique categories and the
corresponding findings of low self-concept.   •

Table 2   Technique of Research, Frequency of Use by Time
          Frame and Corresponding % Low Self-Concept for
          83 Studies.

Technique Category	Frequency of Use and Low Self-Concept Shown as % of Total							
	1939-1953		1954-1963		1964-1973		1939-1973	
	Total Studies	%Low S.C.	Total Studies	%Low S.C.	Total Studies	%Low S.C.	Total Studies	%Low S.C.
I. Forced Choice Identific.	(12)	100%	(5)	100%	(9)	44%	(26)	81%
II. Field Studies	(3)	100%	(1)	0%	(1)	100%	(5)	80%
III. Interviews	(2)	50%	(4)	75%	(4)	100%	(10)	80%
IV. Projective Tests	(1)	100%	(1)	100%	(4)	50%	(6)	67%
V. Self-Concept Scales	(0)	--	(4)	75%	(32)	41%	(36)	44%

Totals   N=18 $\bar{x}$=87.5% N=15 $\bar{x}$=87.5% N=50 $\bar{x}$=83.8% N=83 $\bar{x}$=70.4%

The pattern in Table 2 suggests a link between the kind
of technique used and the frequency of findings of low self-
concept. We note, for example, that when the Forced Choice
Identification Technique is used 81% of these studies over
the total time period 1939-1973 find lower self-concept for
black respondents. This may be contrasted to only 44%
findings of low self-concept for the same time frame when
the Self-Concept Scale Technique is used. One technique,

therefore, is almost twice as likely, to report low self-concept than the other. This observation suggests a need for a more detailed look at the validity of two particular techniques.

Results also appear to be associated with certain common factors such as: the time frame; the geographical representation of the respondents; sample size; the age groupings and frequency of findings of low self-concept. Table 3 below indicates the geographical distribution of the studies and the percent of the total studies reporting low self-concept by time frame.

Table 3   Geographical Distribution by Time Frame for 81 Studies.

Geographic Region	Total Number of Studies and Distribution by Time Frame			
	1939-1953 Total Studies	1954-1963 Total Studies	1964-1973 Total Studies	1939-1973 Total Studies
Northeast	(9) 50%	(4) 25%	(13) 28%	(26) 32%
Southeast	(4) 22%	(11) 69%	(21) 45%	(36) 44%
Midwest & Western	(5) 28%	(1) 6%	(3) 6%	(9) 11%
Cross-sectional	(0) --	(0) --	(10) 21%	(10) 12%
Total	N=18 100%	N=16 100%	N=47 100%	N=81 99%

The relationship between the geographic region from which respondents have been selected and the percentage of the total studies reporting low self-concept is shown by Table 4 on the following page.

Table 4 Geographical Distribution and Percent of Studies Reporting Low Self-Concept for 81 Studies.[1]

Geographic Region	Total Studies and % Reporting Low Self-Concept							
	1939-1953		1954-1963		1964-1973		1939-1973	
	Total Studies	%Low S-C	Total Studies	%Low S-C	Total Studies	%Low S-C	Total Studies	%Low S-C
Northeast	(9)	100%	(4)	100%	(13)	62%	(26)	87%
Southeast	(4)	100%	(11)	80%	(21)	38%	(36)	73%
Midwest & Western	(5)	80%	(1)	100%	(3)	33%	(9)	71%
Cross-Regional	(0)	--	(0)	--	(10)	40%	(10)	40%
Total	N-18	x+93%	N=16	x=93%	N=47	x=43%	N=81	x=67.7%

The studies have most often drawn samples from the
southeastern region with 44% of the total samples coming
from that region. The Northeast is the region from which
the next largest number of samples have been drawn with 32%
the total studies from that region. The Southeastern
and Northeastern regions together account for over three-
fourths of the studies. The remaining studies have drawn
samples almost equally from the combined region of Midwest
and West and Cross-sectional representation.

The distribution of the total subjects per study
ranges between two extremes -- with about ten percent of the

[1]One study represented by Table 4 (above) is not
included in Table 5 because although information for geographic region was provided, the sample size was not
reported.

studies having less than 100 subjects and about ten percent
of the studies having over 1,000 subjects. About eighty
percent of the studies have a total S which ranges in size
from about 101 to 1,000. This distribution allowed for easy
grouping of the studies into subject groupings of small,
medium and large as numerically indicated by Table 5 below.
When we look at the pattern of distribution of low self-
concept by total number of respondents, it appears that
there is no clear association between the total number of
respondents and the frequency of findings of low self-concept.

Table 5. Geographical Distribution, Number of Subjects and
Percent Low Self-Concept for 80 Studies

Geographic Region	Number of Subjects and % Low Self-Concept					
	Small (1-100)	%Low S-C	Medium (101-1,000)	%Low S-C	Large (1,000+)	%Low S-C
Northeast	10	80%	11	90%	5	60%
Southeast	6	66%	26	54%	3	66%
Midwest & Western	2	50%	6	50%	1	100%
Cross-Sectional	0	--	4	75%	6	17%
Total	N=18 x̄=65.3%		N=47 x̄=67.3%		N=15 x̄=60.8%	

From Tables 4 and 5 we observe that fewer studies are
reporting low self-concept as we move forward in time. Some
have speculated that this observed decrease in frequency of
reports of low self-concept among black Americans is related

to increased independence among the African nations, especially during the 1950's and 1960's, as well as to the extensive press given to the 1960 Civil Rights activities and the
accompanying focus upon Black Pride as illustrated by the
slogan "Black is Beautiful." These speculations appear to
be supported by the data of Table 4 which shows a decrease
in the percent of reports finding low self-concept from the
1950's through the 1960's; and by Table 2 which shows a
decrease in reports of low self-concept for these same time
frames irrespective of the technique category used. There
is danger in making this speculation, however, because such
a thesis assumes that prior to these momentous events of the
50's and 60's the Black self-concept was low, or at least
substantially lower than currently reported. This argument
will be developed in more detail in Chapter III.

Another important observation of the data of Tables 4
and 5 is the decrease in frequency of reports of low self-
concept among blacks of the Southeastern as opposed to the
Northeastern geographical regions. This observation has
been made by many investigators (see for example, Wendland
(1967), Baughman (1968, 1971), Powell & Fuller (1973),
Rosenberg and Simmons (1971) and others). This trend towards
higher self-concept among Southwestern blacks compared to
Northeastern blacks may represent different patterns of
reference group and is further considered in the discussion
of reference groups in Chapter III.

As Table 6 which follows indicates, almost one-half
of the studies have focused upon pre-school and elementary
school age children. Although there was a decline in the
relative percent of use of samples drawn from this age group
over the total time frame, this age category has clearly
dominated the self-concept research focus.

Of all of the studies using pre-school and elementary
school age samples, 79% report low self-concept. It is
important to remember, however, that it is among this age
group that the technique of Forced Choice Identification
has most often been used, and that our data clearly indicate
a strong relationship between the use of this technique
and the frequency of findings of low self-concept. It
appears reasonable to conclude that where the Doll Technique
has been used the overall interpretation about findings
about the self-concept of this particular age group should
be open to further investigation. Moreland[1], for example
points out that "Doll Test" studies reporting data about
the self-concept and using samples of pre-school and elementary school children have often not made clear distinctions about the age groupings of the children, and that
his research into the issue indicates some distinctive
patterns which are related to age categories separated into
groups of pre-school children, early school age children

[1]Moreland, J. K. By personal conversation. March,
1974.

and older elementary age school children. The data of
Table 6 also indicates a trend toward high self-concept
among older respondents; however, this may simply reflect
the increased use of self-concept scales.

Table 6   Age Group and Frequency of Findings of Low Self-
Concept for Seventy-Five Studies.

Age Group	Number of Studies and Frequency of Findings of Low Self-Concept as % of Total							
	1939-1953		1954-1963		1964-1973		1939-1973	
	Total Studies	%Low S-C	Total Studies	%Low S-C	Total Studies	%Low S-C	Total Studies	%Low S-C
Pre-School & Elementary	12	92%	6	100%	9	60%	27	79%
Secondary	3	100%	1	100%	8	44%	12	55%
Adult (College & Non-College)	2	100%	3	43%	4	40%	9	47%
Total	F=17	$\bar{x}$=97%	F=10	$\bar{x}$=81%	F=21	$\bar{x}$=48%	F=48	$\bar{x}$=60.3%

The question of possible bias in black self-concept
research resulting from the theoretical orientations linked
to the race-ethnicity of the <u>principal</u> investigator has
received little attention. Perhaps this has been because
principal investigators have often used teams of researchers
for the administration of the measurement or evaluation
insturments and have not necessarily come into direct contact
with the subjects.[1]   It is important to raise the issue

---

[1]The question of the effect of the race of the

however, since it is the principal investigator who estab-
lishes the theoretical orientation of the research and upon
whom the final responsibility rests for the interpretations
and conclusions drawn from the data.

The table below reports the race of the principal
investigators of studies which propose to measure the self-
concepts of Black Americans. Data was obtained for 64 of
the 83 studies (75%) reviewed by this Chapter. Identification of the race of the principal investigator was made
through personal telephone conversations either with the
specific individual, or with individuals who from personal
knowledge were able to make identification for persons
whose names were provided. After the purposes for the inquiry were explained, individuals identified themselves or
their associates as either white or black.

(Continued) administrator of the test instrument upon the
responses of the subjects has received considerable attention. Although numerous articles have been addressed to this
question, and there is a body of empirical studies, there
has been no resolution of the issue in terms of any recognized "best approach." The focus upon the issue has served
to help investigators become sensitive to the possibilities
of influence upon subject responses and race-ethnic bias.
Among the studies we have considered, there appears to be
a general awareness of these possibilities of bias or influence, and the majority of the investigators report either
the use of inter-racial teams of researchers, or the use of
pre-tests to determine the significance of such effects
upon the proposed target group.

Table 7   Race and Total Number of Investigators and %
          Findings of Low Self-Concept for Black Respondents
          for 64 Studies, 1939-1973.

Race of Principal Investigator	Total Number of Investigators Reporting Low Self-Concept Findings and % of Findings of Low Self-Concept for Black Respondents			
	1939-1953 Total %Low Studies S-C	1954-1963 Total %Low Studies S-C	1964-1973 Total %Low Studies S-C	1939-1973 Total %Low Studies S-C
Black	(5) 80%	(2) 100%	(5) 80%	(12) 83% x̄=86
White	(11) 100%	(11) 72%	(30) 45%	(52) 63% x̄=70

        N=16   N=13   N=35   N=64

There appears to be a relationship between the race-ethnicity of the principal investigator and the frequency of findings of low self-concept for black respondents. Black investigators have most often reported low self-concept findings for black Americans and the frequency of such findings is relatively consistent across the total time period. White investigators have reported low self-concepts for black Americans during the earliest time frame; however, with the change in the time frame forward from 1939 to 1973, the frequency of such reported findings decreases significantly.

This tendency of blacks to find low self-concept may be explained by the fact that the self-concept research methodology has been dominated by the techniques of Forced Choice Identification and Field Studies. The studies of the earliest time frame conducted by white investigators reflect a dominant use of the Forced Choice Technique and Projective Tests until about the mid-1950's

when the primary method of self-concept measurement became
the self-concept scale.

The point of particular interest is that although
black investigators have conceptualized the self-concept
to be a global, the measurement instruments most often
used focus upon the single dimension of race/color as the
salient factor from which speculations about the overall
or global self-concept may be made. A review of the literature by time frame, such as provided by the summary chart
of Chapter I, substantiates this observation. (See for
example, Clark and Clark, Frazier, Bayton, Grier and Cobb.)
Several factors should be kept in mind in the interpretation
of this relationship between the race-ethnicity of the
principal investigator and the frequency of findings of
low black self-concepts and the observation that black
investigators have most often reported findings of low self-
concept. Within the black community, stratification by s.e.s.
as well as opportunities for upward mobility either through
employment or marriage (for women) were closely associated with
color during the time periods 1939 through the mid-1950's.[1]
The rigidity of these stratification patterns by color

---

[1] See bibliographic citations to Frazier, Dollard,
Warner, St. Clair, Drake and Kravitz for social history
discussions of this issue.

might well have been the influencing factor which led black
investigators to evaluate a global self-concept in terms of
the perceived salience of the issue of opportunities in the
greater white society in which it was clear that light-
skinned Blacks were preferred for select opportunities.
The number of black investigators of the self-concept of
Black Americans has not increased significantly since 1939
according to the information obtained about race-ethnicity
identity. Since the total numbers of black investigators
are small, there is considerable danger in making speculations about associations between race-ethnicity and frequency of findings of low black self-concept. A more detailed study of the issue could provide significant information concerning the past and present theoretical orientations of blacks and whites engaged in self-concept
research.

In order to have a large body of studies to work
with, the previous analysis has considered a general body
of research which reports about the black self-concept. A
more rigorous analysis may be made, however, when we look
at studies which have administered the same test instrument
to specific populations. A review has been made of a
subset of studies which use specific populations and which
propose to measure and compare the self-concepts of black
and white respondents.

<u>COMPARATIVE STUDIES</u>[1]/

The comparative studies use three techniques for
measurement of the self-concern: (1) Forced Choice Identification (with a focus upon race/color.   (2) Projective
Tests with a focus upon various dimensions through the use
of constructs such as the T.A.T., the Q-Sort and the M.M.P.I.
and the Draw-A-Person Test which is the most frequently
used projective test.   (3) Self-Concept scales which present comparative mean scores for weighted dimensions for
black and white respondents administered the same test.

Table 8 below shows the relative frequency of use
of these three measurement techniques and the reported
levels of black self-concepts compared to whites'.   The
data from these studies present some of the same conflicting

---

[1]/The studies selected for review here are: Horowita
(1939); Helgerson (1943); Goodman (1946); Radke, Trager &
Davis (1949); Radke & Trager (1950); Radke, Southerland &
Rosenberg (1950); Mussen (1953); Landreth & Johnson (1953);
Goodman (1952); Grossack (1955); Moreland (1958); Stevenson
et al. (1958); Moreland (1961); McDonald & Gynther (1962);
Keller (1963); Coleman (1966); Rosenberg (1965); Gregor &
McPherson (1966); Moreland (1965); McDill et al. (1966);
McDonald & Gynther (1965); Larson (1966); Moreland (1966);
Bartee (1967); Gibby & Gabler (1967); Frisch (1967); Wylie
(1967); Yeatts (1967); Baughman (1968); Hodgkins & Stakenas
(1968); Long & Henderson (1968 & 1969); McDonald (1968);
Wendland (1968); Greenwald & Oppenheim (1968); Bridgette
(1968); Asher & Allen (1969); Williams & Byers (1968);
Caplin (1969); Carpenter & Busse (1969); Gordon (1969); Hunt
& Hardt (1969); Epps (1969); Guggeneheim (1969); Kohn &
Schloser (1969); Soares & Soares (1969); Bachman (1970);
Haraba & Grant (1970); Hohnson (1970); Powell & Fuller (1970);
White & Richmond (1970); Hauser (1971); Rosenberg (1971);
Heiss & Owens (1972); Crain & Weisman (1972); Yancy et al.
(1972).

results observed in the larger body of studies. Researchers using the first two techniques almost unanimously report lower black self-concepts compared to whites'. Researchers using the more modern self-concept scales find no difference or higher black self-concepts compared to whites'.

Table 8 Levels of Black Self-Concept Compared to Whites' For 59 Studies, 1939-1973.

Technique Category	Frequency of Technique and Level of Black Self-Concept Compared to Whites'											
	1939-1953			1954-1963			1964-1973			1939-1973		
	Hi	Lo	ND	Hi	Lo	ND	Hi	Lo	ND	Hi	Lo	ND
I. Forced Choice Identification	–	(10) 100%		–	(3) 100%	–	–	(5) 56%	(4) 45%	–	(18) 82%	(4) 18%
II. Projective Tests	–	(2) 100%	–	–	(2) 100%	–	–	(5) 100%	–	–	(9) 100%	–
III. Self-Concept Scales	–	–	–	–	(1) 100%	–	(11) 42%	(5) 19%	(10) 34%	(11) 41%	(6) 22%	(10) 38%

$$N=12 \qquad N=6 \qquad N=40 \qquad N=58$$

Throughout this review of the research we have found irregular patterns of results. There have even been differing reports about levels of black self-concept among studies reporting the use of the same instrument with comparable specific populations.[1]

Thus far, this review has focused upon the relationship between selected variables and the frequency of findings

---

[1] See for example Bridgette (1968) and Wendland (1968).

of low self-concept. We have found that there appears to be an association between findings of low self-concept and the time frame of the study; the research technique used and the geographical representation of the sample. The data indicate that findings of low self-concept are most closely associated with the Forced Choice Identification Technique, and the preschool and elementary school age group. Moreover, there appears to be a greater report of low self-concept among studies selecting Northeastern as opposed to Southeastern subjects. The extreme variability of these findings leads us to conclude that researchers have been studying a widely shifting phenomenon or that there are serious validity problems in the study of the self-concept. We suspect the latter and shall, therefore, consider some problems in the measurement of self-concept. In the next Chapter, we shall look at changes in the definition of self-concept for a body of studies.

PROBLEMS IN THE MEASUREMENT OF SELF-CONCEPT:

The problem of the measurement of the self-concept might best be considered through attention to two measurement techniques most often used by the researcher:

(I) The Forced Choice Identification Technique and

(II) Self-Concept Scales.

A. The Forced Choice Technique:

The Forced Choice Technique was first used by Horowitz in 1939 and then used and extended in its scope by

s such as Clark and Clark (1939, 1940, 1947); Helgerson
(1943); Goodman (1946); and others. Primarily, the technique was developed as a means for measuring or determining
race awareness among young children. Although the earliest
uses of the technique focused upon the age of awareness of
race-color, it appears that the technique became a means
for the measurement of self-esteem when it was observed
that black children consistently selected white dolls in
response to the request situations and in interview sessions
expressed many of the dominant white stereotype attitudes
towards the black doll.

With a growing awareness of these observations among
those using the "Doll Test" technique there appears to have
developed an accompanying theoretical orientation, discussed earlier in Chapter I, which supported the thesis
that the rejection of black dolls by black children was
indicative of the "Black pathology" (preference for white
and rejection of black, and identification with the op-
pressor).

Several questions must be answered with respect to
the face validity of the "Doll Test". First, the extent
to which color-race awareness and preference for light
skin is a viable indication of self-concept is questionable.
As previously mentioned, when children have been requested
to make choices between black and white dolls which are
identical in every manner except skin color, the black

children are reported to select to a statistically significant degree (compared to matched white groups) white dolls
and to reject black dolls. Also, when the technique has
been used in modified form and children have been requested
to assign roles and social status to the dolls or doll families, it has been observed that black children have consistently assigned low status and social situations to
black dolls and have associated with the black dolls many
of the majority white group stereotypes about Blacks. What
is questionable, however, is the extent to which the preference for white dolls is an indication of low self-concept as
opposed to the children's realistic awareness of institutionalized racism as it continues to exist in America.

It has been reported, for example, that young children both black and white in grades 3-12 have an awareness
of status consciousness and which clearly reflects the adult
majority. Simmons reports the following about his study of
1,917 children from a Baltimore City:

> . . . as early as the elementary school state,
> children rate occupations in an order almost
> identical to that of high school pupils, and
> indeed, of adult samples.

Of particular interest is the report by the author that:

> . . . the children, both younger and older do not
> appear to accept the doctrine of equality of op-
> portunity . . . those who do have an opinion al-
> most always believe equal opportunity to be blocked
> to some types of children. Seventy percent of
> those elementary school children who understood
> the question (Do all kids in America have the same
> chance to grow up and get the good things in life,
> or Do some kids not have as good a chance as others,

> or Don't you know.) believe that some kids
> do <u>not</u> have as good a chance as others . . .
> Of those children who indicate what type of
> children do not have an equal chance, 68% attri-
> bute the problem explicitly to socioeconomic,
> racial, or ethnic disadvantages . . . Many young
> children seem to be as perceptive about the Amer-
> ican opportunity structure as they are about the
> prestige hierarchy.[1]

In rejecting black dolls and the accompanying low status
assignments, the black child could be reflecting his rejection of the perceived low status assignments to him by this
greater society but not his own personal rejection of himself.

Some question might also be raised about the character
of the test materials used in the Doll Test. Of particular
interest is the early study use of identical black and white
dolls, doll families and puppets. During the early time
frame and on into the middle time frame when the Forced
Choice Technique were frequently used there were very
limited numbers of black dolls on the market and probably
fewer numbers of doll families and playhouses. Those dolls
that were available were most often of the exaggerated
"topsi" or "Kewpie" type. One might seriously question the

Simmons, Roberta G. and Morris Rosenberg. "Functions of Children's Perceptions of the Stratification System." American Sociological Review, V. 36, no. 1-3, 1971:
235-249. For some further related discussion see: "The
Experimentally-Increased Salience of Extreme Comparative
Reference Groups," by Robert G. Simmons. Sociology and
Social Research, V. 53, 1968-69: 490-497.

extent to which a white a white doll painted black ade-
quately suggests self-identification to a black child.[1]

    B. Self-Concept Scales

    One of the most recent and detailed evaluations of
self-concept scales has been prepared by Rick Crandall.[2]
In a discussion about the validity of self-concept constructs
he writes:

> . . . Because of the general lack of psycho-
> metric work in this area it is easy to be
> critical of all existing measures . . . val-
> idation data are largely missing in the self-
> concept area . . . Most of us would probably
> prefer to use an existing measure rather than
> spend <u>years</u> necessary to fully validate a
> measure for use . . . Because in many cases
> we can still get results using imperfect
> measures and because the lack of outstanding
> measures may tempt people to construct their
> own measures validity work tends to be ig-
> nored.[1]

    Crandall provides a ranking of the self-concept scales
which have either been used more than once in published reports or which according to the evaluation tests have "po-
tential for further development." He presents a detailed
consideration of some thirty-three self-concept scales
found in the relatively recent literature and he offers a

---

[1]Black dolls historically have enjoyed their most
favorable market (1) during the main thrust of the Garvey
movement and (2) during the more recent re-focus upon
"Black is beautiful."

[2]Crandall, Rick. "The Measurement of Self-Esteem
and Related Constructs" in <u>Measures of Social Psychological
Attitudes</u> by J. Robinson and P. Sharer. Institute for Social
Research, University of Michigan, 1973: 45-158.

ranking of the top eight scales. With respect to this
ranking, he states:

> . . . The first eight scales, . . . represent
> the best of the current scales specifically de-
> signed to measure self-esteem. The next . . .
> represent measures which have less validation
> work. Most of these could become important
> scales with additional validation work.[1]

The top eight scales, as ranked by Crandall are:

1. The Tennessee Self-Concept Scale (Pitts 1964)

2. The Piers-Harris Children's Self-Concept Scale

3. The Janis-Field Feelings of Inadequacy Scale
   (Eagly 1967)

4. Self-Esteem Scale (Rosenberg 1965)

5. Self-Esteem Inventory (Coopersmith 1967)

6. The Index of Adjustment and Values (Bills et al.
   1961)

7. The Butler-Haigh Q-Sort (Butler and Haigh 1954)

8. The Miskimins Self-Goal-Other Discrepancy Scale
   (Miskimins 1971)

Let us use Crandall's rank order of preference for
self-concept scales and determine the use of these scales
among the studies of concern to us. Further, let us observe
with respect to these scales, the frequency of their use
among the studies and the reported self-concept. In our consideration, we shall select only those studies where specific
reference is made to the scale by exact name and where the
scale is the primary instrument for the measurement of
self-concept for the study.

---

[1]Crandall, Rick. op. cit.

A review of the studies reveals that only three of
these top eight ranked scales are identifiable among the
eighty-two studies presented here. The three scales used
are presented in the order of their frequency of use with
the corresponding finding of low self-concept in Table 7
below:

Table 7 Frequency of Use and Finding of Low Self-Concept
for Three Top-Ranked Self-Concept Scales Among
Eighty-Two Studies.

Crandall's Scale and Title of Scale Rank Order	Frequency of Use	%Low S-C
#1 Tenn. Self-Concept (Pitts)	6	(4) 67%
#2 Rosenberg Self-Esteem	6	(2) 33%
#3 Coopersmith Self-Esteem	2	(1) 50%
Totals	F=14	$\bar{x}$=50%

The Tennessee Self-Concept Scale, contains ninety
statements which represent fifteen categories which fall into
five general areas: (1) the physical self (2) the moral-
ethical self (3) the personal self (4) family self and
(5) the social self. The Coopersmith Self-Esteem Inventory
also evaluates attitudes towards the self in several areas:
(1) self-derogation (2) leadership-popularity (3) family-
parents and (4) assertiveness. The Rosenberg Self-Esteem
Scale is primarily designed to measure the self-acceptance
factor of self-esteem; which reflects his thesis that one's

total self-acceptance is indicative of one's self-concept.
All of the items of the Rosenberg Scale are concerned with
liking or approving the self.

The validity of these scales has been carefully
outlined by Crandall as well as by the principal authors in
their respective publications. Crandall reports the following about the validation of the scales:

> "The Tennessee Self-Concept Scale has norms based
> on 626 people from ages 12-68 and has a test-retest
> reliability of . . . 92, with a test-retest reli-
> ability of various subscores ranging between .70
> and .90.
>
> The Rosenberg Self-Esteem Scale was normalized for
> a sample of 5,024 junior and senior high school
> students from ten randomly selected schools in
> New York.
>
> The Coopersmith Self-Esteem Inventory was normal-
> ized for 220 male 5th and 6th graders of middle
> class Ses. The test-retest reliability for the
> original scale was .88 over five weeks and .70
> over seven years.[1]

These three scales appear to provide the most rigorous methodological approaches to the measurement of the
self-concept among the studies which have been of interest
to us in this Chapter. In the 14 studies in which they
were used, one-half found low black self-concept and the
other one-half found either no difference or higher black
self-concepts. This analysis reinforces our earlier conclusion that generalizations about low self-concepts are
highly questionable.

---

[1]Crandall, R., op. cit.

Conclusion:

The patterns of conflicting findings analyzed in these chapters makes generalized statements about low black self-concept highly questionable. The study results, taken as a whole, appear to be largely a function of the research instrument used; the theoretical orientation of the researcher and time and place of study. Psychiatrists, convinced of damaged Black psyches, find low self-concepts; while researchers less convinced of the psychic damage done by slavery and segregation find healthy black self-concepts.

This Chapter has suggested that this conflict of findings indicates validity problems. It appears that the notion of just what a "self-concept" is has been poorly conceptualized, and further, that serious problems exist in measuring self-concept, once defined. We have analyzed some of these measurement problems, and in the next Chapter shall consider problems in the conceptualization of self-concept.

CHAPTER III

Theoretical Orientations And Directions for Continued Black
Self-Concept Research

This Chapter examines differences in the way self-
concept has been conceptualized, and suggests that self-
concept is a much more complex and subtle cognitive phenomenon than most of the research indicates. Specifically, we
shall argue that the self-concept is multidimensional, specific and comparative and thus variable by situation. This
theoretical orientation suggests some directions for future
research and social policy.

Definitions of Self-Concept

Few of the studies present clear definitions of self-
concept; rather in the large majority of instances, the way
self-concept is conceptualized must be inferred from the
methodology. To arrive at a definition of the self-concept
being measured, one has to do a certain amount of reasoning
backwards; that is, one has to look at the measurement instrument used to determine the definition of the self-concept
which the investigator had in mind. This endeavor has not
always been easy, and perhaps more than anything serves to
illustrate how uncertain many of the researchers are about
the phenomenon. While researchers have all conceptualized
the self-concept to be a set of cognitive elements, they
vary according to whether they consider self-concept to be:

(1) unidimensional or multidimentional (2) situational or
non-situational.

Is the Self-Concept Unidimensional or Multidimensional?

Self-concept have been viewed by some as unidimensional. Studies using the Doll Test for the measurement of
self-concept have presumed that color represented the single
dimension of self-evaluation regardless of other factors
of interaction or the situation. For illustration, let us
consider a college student (CS) and assume that he is a
good student and a good athlete. Also, let us assume that
CS is popular with his peers and is president of his class,
because he is also a good leader. We might well assume
that CS has a high self-concept because of these abilities
and accomplishments.

If our subject is black, however, following the
logic suggested by the Doll Tests, we would assume that CS
has a unidimensional self-concept (color-race) which dominates
his evaluation of himself regardless of other factors. CS
then becomes the smart black student; the good black athlete,
the popular black student who is president of his class, etc.
In short, we presume that CS perceives himself as black CS.
If we were to measure CS's feeling about color and find that
he expresses a preference for white skin, we would conclude
that CS has a low self-concept.

This example clearly illustrates the absurdity of
such a conceptualization; rather, it is much more likely

that CS and other individuals preceive themselves in terms
of many dimensions, some of which we have already mentioned:
the physical self, the social self, the academic self.
Various situations are likely to elicit particular dimensions for self assessment. If we were to ask CS if he is
a good athlete, we might expect him to say yes, and to have
a high self-concept. If we were to ask him if he is a good
student, or if he is popular with his classmates, he would
say yes and we might expect him to have a high self-concept.
However, it might be that CS does not relate to his family
very well, and if we were to ask him about his family relationship, on that dimension we might expect him to have a
low self-concept. In sum, CS would fluctuate in his self-
concept according to a number of dimensions.

The question which immediately comes to mind is just
how general these dimensions are. Let us again return to
CS to illustrate the degrees of generality of specificity of
the self-concept. We might ask CS about his academic self-
concept and decide upon learning that his grades are B's
that he is a good student. On the other hand, we might wish
to evaluate a more specific self-concept and could therefore ask CS if he is a good English student. CS could
respond that since he has a B average, he is a good English
student. We could decide that we want to be even more
specific and press CS into revealing that although he has a
B average in English and an excellent reading speed, he is a

very poor speller; or that although he is outstanding in
English literature, he has a limited mastery of grammar. Our
evaluation of CS would have proceeded from assessments of
a very general academic self-concept to specific assessments
of ability. CS's responses would represent his academic
self-concept along increasingly specific dimensions.

Many researchers have indicated that they consider
self-concept to be multidimensional, but also they suggest
a general global self-concept which is held by the individual.
This global self-concept is often conceptualized to be the
mean of the individual's evaluation of himself along several
general dimensions and to be carried about by the individual
through all situations. An individual could conceivably
decide that on a scale from 1 to 10, he is 1 in athletics;
5 in sociability; 6 in attractiveness and 10 in his academic
performance. He is therefore a 5.5, which is his mean self-
concept. Later we will review some evidence which leads us
to doubt the importance of this "global" self-concept.

Is the Self-Concept Situational or Non-Situational?

Although CS might be tired of talking to us by now,
he may allow us to continue to try to determine something
about his self-concept. With reference group theory in
mind, we might begin a new line of inquiry. Previously, we
have noted that CS has indicated that he is a good athlete.
We might now mention to him that a student from another
campus will be the U. S. Olympic representative in the

Decathalon competitions, and after making this observation,
we might again inquire about CS's athletic self-concept.
This time, CS might indicate that he is the best athlete on
his campus (thereby suggesting that other athletes on his
campus provide his comparative reference group and not the
Olympic representative we have mentioned); or, CS might
indicate that if he had more time to practice, he could be
as good an athlete as the Olympic representative we have
mentioned (thereby suggesting that he is using the standards
of performance of the young man we mentioned as his comparative reference). During the course of our conversation about
his athletic ability, CS would have indicated a change in
comparative reference groups.

The possibility of change in reference groups has not
often been considered by researchers conducting black self-
concept research. This lack of attention to reference
groups can present complex problems of interpretation of
self-concept findings. One such problem comes from semantic
differences between subcultures. Consider for example,
two   self-concept scales previously discussed (Tennessee
and Ronenberg). If we evaluate statements from
these scales with respect to reference groups, we immediately
encounter difficulty. Let us select several for illustration:

"I am a bad person." (Tennessee)

"I am proud of my school work." (Rosenberg)
Further, let us assume that the test is given in school, and
that the test is being taken by a black student in a

predominantly white school. What is the frame of reference for the student? From the point of view of semantics, the question of being a bad person presents problems, since often being bad is good. Consider if you will that a "bad cat" might do all the right things: he is attractive, he dresses well, he is a good student, a good athlete, popular, and able to take care of himself. In terms of semantics, it is precisely because he is so good that he is bad. Now granted that all of this is true, when the Black student, for whom these semantics are relevant, faces this statement in the school situation outlined above, he must first stop and consider the reference group. Is the subject to assume that the question on value reflects the normative standards of the school (the in-school triggered test situation), in which case he might well be considered to behave badly by the teachers; or is he to assume that the question relates to the perception of himself by his peer group (he is bad because he fights all of the time and is a bully, or is he bad in terms of the good bad).

From the point of the comparative reference group is the subject to evaluate himself in terms of most of his classmates (which in this situation would be predominantly white); or in terms of his interaction group (which is likely to be black). What is lacking is the guide which would help the subject interpret the question and the researcher interpret the answer: such as, compared to my friends with whom I play when not in school, I am a bad person, or some similar construction.

Some of the same problems exist with respect to the statement: "I am proud of my school work." Suppose that the subject's interaction group does not place a value upon education; specifically, they believe that one should not do well in school but rather defy the teacher and give little attention to learning. When the subject is faced with the above question, and he knows that his school work is below standard (suggested by the teacher), is he to respond in terms of pride because of the norms of his interaction group, or should he respond in terms of embarrassment about his low academic performance because of the norms of the teacher.

Possibly our subject is from a neighborhood where the schools are said to be very poor and although his grades are just average, he places a high value upon education. In response to the question about pride in his school work, is he to respond in terms of pride (assuming that the standards of his school are higher than those of his neighborhood) or in terms of embarrassment because he is not doing as well as the top half of the students in his class? Moreover, if the subject's school work is known to him to have improved over the past semester, is he to be proud (because of the improvement) or embarrassed (because he is not in the top half of his class)?

For a student who makes good grades, a test given in one of the classrooms might trigger his positive feelings about his academic ability and his responses to self-concept test inquiries might reflect that trend of thought. For a poor student who does only what is necessary to make grades good enough to allow him to play ball, the trend of thought might be that the test is not important to his interests, and he might reflect an uncertainty about whether his reference should be how he performs or how he could perform if it were important to him. In a similar manner, if the test is given in the school gymnasium, or the school cafeteria, two favorite places for the administration of tests to large numbers of students, various references might be suggested to various students. Given this in-school test situation, the researcher must therefore evaluate the test results with a careful eye upon the possibility of bias. Clearly, the test situation in the classroom as opposed to some setting which elicits different definitions must be considered in informed self-concept methodologies. Most of the general studies about black self-concepts have been conducted in school situations, and often the administration of the measurement instrument has been through the assistance of classroom teachers, guidance counselors, or various other school personnel. Such school personnel are traditionally identified with a specific set or norms for behavior as well as academic performance. All too often because of a failure to provide a means for identification of reference groups within the measurement construct, results of measurements of black self-concept are evaluated on the basis of the cultural or race-ethnic orientation of the investigator.

What Kind of Self-Concept Does The Evidence Support?

Most of the research that considers self-concept to be global reports lower self-concepts for blacks than whites; however, little work has demonstrated behavioral correlates of this so-called global self. Also indicators of this global self are seldomly highly correlate. For these reasons we suspect the existence of such global cognitions is questionable. Rather, it is much more likely the global self-concepts are artifacts of the research methodologies. More specifically a careful reading of the research suggests low black global self concepts is an artifact of two important specific dimensions on which blacks do appear to be lower than whites. The first is color preference, which has been discussed above. The second dimension is one frequently not recognized in self-concept research, but when made explicit appears extremely important. This important and perpetually hidden dimension has been labelled by Gurin and Gurin as internal/external control.[1]

The Gurin and Gurin findings appear to have been neglected by many conducting black self-concept research. Attention to the internal/external control dimension provides insight into the frequency with which blacks are reported to have lower self-concepts than whites. In the past, whites have tended to show preferences for blacks with lighter skin

---

[1]Gurin, Patricia, et al. "Internal-External Control in the Motivational Dynamics of Negro Youth," Journal of Social Issues, V. 25, no. 8, Summer 1969, p. 29-51.

color; consequently, these individuals have held positions
which have offered opportunities for upward mobility. There
has been a tendency for blacks to select light skin colors;
however, it appears that such patterns have been related to
the associated opportunities for upward mobility, power, and
status.

In a very well know study of school children across
the nation that has come to be know as "The Coleman Report,"
James Coleman and associates presented findings which show
blacks to be lower than whites on the dimension of internal/
external control. For a large nationwide sample of 6th, 9th,
and 12th grade students he reports that:

> ". . . both Negro and white children expressed a
> high [academic] self-concept, as well as high in-
> terest in school and learning, compared to the
> other [ethnic] groups. Negroes, however, were like
> the other minority groups in expressing a much
> lower sense of control over the environment than
> whites.
> . . . For the child's sense of control over the
> environment, there is in addition a consistent
> relation to the economic level of the home and the
> structural integrity of the home. That is, chil-
> dren from homes where the father is present, show
> a higher sense of control of the environment than
> do children from homes with lower economic level
> or children from homes where the father is absent."[1]

The importance of the underlying dimension of
internal/external control is illustrated by the Lorenz (1960)
study of segregated and integrated projects in New York. He
found that blacks in integrated projects had higher "self-
esteem" than whites. These findings indicated to him that

[1] Coleman, James. Equality of Educational Opportunity. U.S.
Office of Education, Washington, D.C., 1966.

the project represented upward mobility for the blacks and
downward mobility for the whites. Black residents were reported to have confidence about their upward mobility but
uncertainties about their ability to assure upward mobility
for their children. These observations by Lorenz suggest
that what was actually being measured was not a global self-
concept (self-esteem) but two specific dimensions of self-
concept: (1) the individual's perception of opportunity for
upward mobility for himself (concept of ability) and (2) the
individual's perception of his ability to control factors
which would allow him to provide greater opportunities for
his children, in other words, internal/external control.

The same interpretation can be made of the Haggstrom
and Conrad study (1962) of thirty desegregated and thirty
matched segregated households in Detroit. They found that
the members of the desegregated households tended to have
higher self-esteem than matched members of segregated households. Whereas the authors speculated that the black community "depressed" the self-esteem of its members, what is
more likely being measured is not a general "self-esteem"
but internal/external control.

The view that self-concept is a multidimensional,
specific phenomenon which changes with reference groups is
supported by the evidence, although usually the investigators
have not had such a conceptualization in mind. Let us look
at several studies which compare the self-concept of black
and white respondents and report findings which suggest that

the black self-concept has changed as comparative reference groups have changed.

Two schools of thought about the comparative reference groups of blacks in integrated as opposed to segregated schools have developed. One school (closely associated with Thomas Pettigrew) suggests that the black student in the integrated school has low self-concepts because he compares himself to white students.[1] The other school (closely associated with James Coleman) suggests that the black student in integrated schools has a high self-concept because he compares himself with black students in segregated schools.[2] The evidence is mixed. Williams and Byers (1968) reported no difference between the self-esteem for blacks in integrated schools and segregated schools. White and Richmond (1970) found the same thing for a sample of black 5th graders from economically advantaged predominantly white schools compared to a matched sample of economically deprived black students in predominantly black schools.

On the other hand, Powell and Fuller (1970) in a study of the psychological impact of school desegregation on 7th, 8th, and 9th graders in a southern city found integration lowered self-concept. Although black students in both

---

[1] Pettigrew, Thomas F. Racially Separate or Together?, New York: McGraw-Hill, 1971.

[2] Coleman, James. Equality of Educational Opportunity. U. S. Office of Education, Washington, D. C., 1966.

integrated and segregated schools had higher self-concepts scores than whites, the black students in segregated or predominantly black schools achieved the highest self-concept scores. The researchers suggested that the higher self-concepts of the segregated blacks reflected their pride in their own community; the influence of black success models and to a certain degree the respondents insulation from the devalued view of blacks by the white majority. A more viable explanation is that these self-concept scores simply reflect differences in reference groups. Regardless of which of the schools of thought one supports about the <u>direction</u> of change in the black self-concept in integrated as opposed to seg-. regated schools, it is very likely that these studies are measuring a change in the comparative reference group.

Different Conceptualizations of Self-Concept And The Accompanying Findings.

The above discussions suggest a need to look at the data for the comparative studies discussed in Chapter II to see what has happened to reported findings about black and white self-concepts when different definitions have been used. Table 8 presents this information.

Table 8. The Relationship Between How Self-Concept Has Been
Conceptualized And Research Findings Reported For
Blacks Compared To Whites.

Conceptualization of Self-Concept	Frequency of Use by Category and % of Studies Reporting Various Levels of Black Self-Concept Compared to Whites'											
	1939-1953			1954-1963			1964-1973			1939-1973		
	Hi	Lo	ND	Hi	Lo	ND	Hi	Lo	ND	Hi	Lo	ND
Category 1: Global based on a single dimension.	-	(1?) 100%	-	-	(3) 100%	-	-	(5) 56%	(4) 45%	-	(8) 82%	(4) 18%
Category 2: Global based on multidimensions.	--	(2) 100%	-	-	(3) 100%	-	(10) 40%	(10) 40%	(5) 20%	(10) 33%	(15?) 50%	(5) 17%
Category 3: Multidimensional and situational	-	-	-	-	-	-	(1) 17%	-	(5) 83%	(1) 17%	--	(5) 83%
	N=12			N=16			N=40			N=58		

Table 8 indicates that when the self-concept has
been defined to be global based on a single dimension, the
black self-concept compared to whites' has been very low; however when the conceptionalized self-concept has been global
based upon several dimensions the difference between black and
white self-concepts diminishes. This pattern primarily reflects the methods for measurement of the self-concept which
has accompanied the conceptualization. For all of the studies
grouped under Category 1, the Forced Choice Technique has been
used. The methodologies used by the studies falling into
Category 2 have included projective tests and multidimensional
self-concept scales. Since the number of tests using scales
far exceeds the number of tests using projective techniques,

we may conclude that approaches to self-concept measurement
which allow for dimensions other than color-race report findings for the black self-concept which are very different from
those of Category 1. When the self-concept has been conceptualized to be situational, the definition category which we
consider to be most viable, the self-concept measured has
been specific and self-concept have been essentially no different. Among the studies grouped into Category 3, however,
the dimension measured has been either a general academic
self-concept (see for example, Coleman)[1] or a more specific
academic concept stated as the concept of ability (see
Wylie.)[2]

---

[1]Op. cit.

[2]Wylie, Ruth C. "Schoolwork-Ability. Estimates
and Aspirations as a Function of Socioeconomic Level, Race
and Sex," Psychological Report. Vol. 21, 1967, 781-808.

Conclusions and Policy Implications.

   Perhaps the Cooley-Mead tradition in social psychology
has led to an underestimation of the complexity and subtle-
ties in the cognitive distinctions human beings are capable
of making. The research of black self-concept sheds doubt
on whether individuals actually form global, non-situational
self-concepts; rather, they evaluate themselves along
specific dimensions in comparison with others.

   When blacks compare themselves to whites they appear
generally to have lower self-concepts on the specific dimensions:
color preference and inter/external control. It has been
suggested that these two dimensions are very closely related
and that color preference is a product of the perception of
internal/external control. That these dimensions are low
for blacks compared to whites appears to be a function of
white racism as it has come to be institutionalized. Summary
statements of global self-concepts are often artifacts of
studies of these heavily weighted dimensions.

   The slogan "Black is Beautiful" symbolizes a collec-
tive movement which has done much to bring about changes in
patterns of reward based upon color. The slogan has served
both blacks and whites. It has effected the thinking of the
white community, resulting in some visible changes in patterns
of employment and related opportunities for blacks. Tele-
vision, movies and magazines, for example, in an effort to
use "visible" blacks have come to use easily visible blacks

(dark blacks). As the attitudes and behavior of White
America become increasingly positive and apparent to Black
America, we might expect changes in a positive direction for
blacks low on internal/external control.[1]/

The "Black is Beautiful" movement has been influen-
tial, in many direct and indirect ways, in changing some
dimensions of the black self-concept, espeically color preference. However, there is danger in building programs
which can do little to effect the black self-concept on
other specific dimensions which are vital to life chances.
A "beautiful" black athlete who fails his course of study is
little helped by programs which continue to assume that if
only he would choose the black doll he would be all right.
What that beautiful individual might need is a specific
program which increases his possiblity for academic success
and the accompanying opportunities for employment. Or, what
that individual might need is a specific program through
which he is able to better understand the national political
and economic structure, and means through which long-term
effective changes may be made in the interest of the disadvantaged. It remains a reality that in most of his interaction with whites, the black is engaging in activities
which require abilities more widely held by whites than

---

[1]/Racial Attitudes in School Children: From Kinder-
garten Through High School. U. S. Office of Education,
Washington, D. C., 1972. [Project No. 2-C-009, Grant No.
OEG-3-72-0014]

blacks. The problem produced by low self-concept in these situations will continue to plague blacks no matter how beautiful they may be.

Guidelines for social policy might be obtained from continued study of the black self-concept, especially those studies which give closer attention to situations which effect the self-concept on specific dimensions. The accompanying challenge to continued black self-concept study is evident. Sociologists engaged in such research need to be sure that self-concept research not only continues to examine the antecedents of self-concept, but also to consider the self in social interaction.

BIBLIOGRAPHY

Asher, Steven R. and Vernon L. Allen. "Racial Preference
    1969 and Social Comparison Process," Journal of
          Social Issues, XXV, No. 1 (1969), 157-166.

Bachman, Jerald G. Youth in Transition, Vol. II: The
    1970 Impact of Family Background and Intelligence
          on Tenth-Grade Boys. Ann Arbor, Michigan:
          Survey Research Center, Institute for Social
          Research, 1970.

Banks, James A. and Jean D. Grambs. Black Self-Concept
    1972 New York: McGraw-Hill Book Co., 1972.

Bartee, Geraldine M. "The Perceptual Characteristics of
    1967 Disadvantaged Negro and Caucasian College Students,"
          unpublished Ph.D. dissertation, East Texas
          State University, 1967.

Bass, Edwin J. "An Investigation of Changes in Selected
    1969 Ninth Grade Students' Concepts of Self and of
          Others After Interaction With Selected Materials
          Taught in Integrated and Segregated Groups,"
          Dissertation Abstracts, v. 29 (1969), 2991-A-
          2992-A.

Baughman, E. Earl. Black Americans. A Psychological
    1971 Analysis. New York: Academic Press, 1971.

Baughman, E. Earl and W. Grant Dahlstrom. Negro and White
    1968 Children: A Psychological Study in the Rural
          South. New York: Academic Press, 1968.

Bayton, James A., et al. "Negro Perception of Negro and
    1965 White Personality Traits," Journal of Personality
          and Social Psychology, I, No. 3 (1965), 250-253.

Bem, Daryl. Beliefs, Attitudes, and Human Affairs. Belmont,
    1970 Calif.: Brooks-Cole Publishing Co., 1970. [Chapters
          5, 6, and 7.]

Benvenu, M. "Effects of School Integration on The Self-
    1968 Concept and Anxiety of Lower-Class, Negro Adolescent
          Males," Dissertation Abstract, v. 29 (1968), 629-A.

Blalock, Hubert M. and Ann B. Blalock. Methodology in Social
    1968 Research. New York: McGraw-Hill Co., 1968.

Boyd, George Felix. "The Levels of Aspiration of White
    1952   and Negro Children in a Non-Segregated Elementary
           School," The Journal of Social Psychology, 36
           (1952), 191-196.

Brazziel, William F. "Correlates of Southern Negro
    1963   Personality," Journal of Negro Education, (1963)
           46-53.

Bridgette, Richard E. "Self-Esteem in Negro and White
    1968   Southern Adolescents," unpublished paper,
           University of North Carolina, 1968.

Brody, Eugene B. "Marginality, Identity and Behavior in
    1964   the American Negro: A Functional Analysis,"
           International Journal of Social Psychiatry, 10,
           1964, 7-12.

Butts, Hugh F. "Skin Color Perception and Self-Esteem,"
    1963   Journal of Negro Education, XXXII (1963), 122-129.

Caplin, Morris D. "The Relationship Between Self-Concept
    1969   and Academic Achievement," Journal of Experimental
           Education, v. 37, No. 3 (Spring 1969), 12-14.

Carpenter, T. R. and T. V. Busse. "Development of Self-
    1969   Concept In Negro and White Welfare Children,"
           Child Development, v. 40 (1969), 935-939.

Chethiik, M. "A Quest for Identity: Treatment of
    1967   Disturbed Negro Children In A Predominantly
           White Center," American Journal of Orthopsychiatry,
           v. 37 (1967), 71-77.

Clark, Kenneth. Dark Ghetto. Dilemmas of Social Power.
    1965   New York: Harper & Row, 1965.

Clark, Kenneth B. and Mamie P. Clark. "The Development of
    1939   Consciousness of Self and the Emergence of Racial
           Identification in Negro Preschool Children,"
           Journal of Social Psychology (1939), 591-599.

_____. "Racial Identification
    1952   and Preference in Negro Children," in Readings in
           Social Psychology. New York: Holt and Co., (1952),
           551-560.

_____. "Skin Color As A
    1940   Factor in Racial Identification of Negro Preschool
           Children," Journal of Social Psychology, S.P.S.I.I.
           Bulletin (1940), II, 159-169.

-105-

Coleman, et al. "Focus of Control and Academic Performance
1966 Among Racial Groups," Equality of Educational
Opportunity. Washington, D.C., Government
Printing Office, 1966.

Coles, Robert. Children of Crisis: A Study of Courage
1964 and Fear. New York: Dell Publishing Co., 1964.

Cooley, Charles H. Human Nature and the Social Order.
1970 New York: Schocken Books, 1970.

Coppersmith, Stanley. The Antecedents of Self-Esteem. San
1967 Francisco: W. H. Freeman & Co., 1967.

Crain, Robert L. and Carol S. Weisman. Discrimination,
1972 Personality and Achievement. New York: Seminar
Press, 1972.

Crandall, Rich and A. P. McDonald, Jr. Measures of Self-
1973 Esteem; Measures of Internal-External Control.
Ann Arbor, Mich.: Institute for Social Research,
1973. Supplement and revisions of chapters for
Measures of Social Psychological Attitudes.

Davis, Allison, and John Dollard. Children of Bondage.
1940 The Personality Development of Negro Youth in the
Urban South. New York: Harper & Row, 1940.
(Selected case studies.)

_____. Children of Bondage.
1964 New York: Harper and Row, 1964. (Originally
published in 1940 by The American Council on
Education, Washington, D.C.)

Dollard, John. Caste and Class in a Southern Town. New
1937 York: Doubleday Anchor Books, 1937.

Dreger, R. M. and K. S. Miller. "Comparative Psychological
1960 Studies of Negroes and Whites in the United States."
Psychological Bulletin, LVI (1960), 361-402.

Epps, Edgar G. "Correlates of Academic Achievement Among
1969 Northern and Southern Urban Negro Students,"
Journal of Social Issues, XXV, No. 3 (1969), 55-68.

Erickson, Erik. "The Concept of Identity." Daedalus
1966 (Winter 1966), 145-171.

Forward, John R. and J. R. Williams. "Internal-External
1967 Control and Black Militancy," Journal of Social
Issues, XXVI, No. 1 (1967), 75-92.

Franklin, John Hope. ed. Color and Race. Boston: Beacon
1968 Press, 1968.

Franklin, John Hope. From Slavery to Freedom. A History
1967 of the Negro in America. New York: Vintage Books,
1967.

Frazier, E. Franklin. Black Bourgeoisie. The Rise of a
1957 New Middle Class. London: Collier-MacMillan, Ltd.,
1957.

Frazier, Franklin E. Negro Youth At The Crossways. New
1967 York: Schocken Books, 1967. (Originally
published in 1940 by The American Council on
Education, Washington, D.C.)

Frisch, Gloria and L. Handler. "Differences in Negro and
1967 White Drawings: A Cultural Interpretation,"
Perceptual and Motor Skills, v. 24 (1967), 667-670.

Georgeoff, P. "The Elementary Curriculum as a Factor in
1972 Racial Understanding," In J. A. Banks and J. D.
Grambs, Black Self-Concept: Implications for
Education and Social Science, McGraw-Hill Co.,
(1972), 94.

Gergen, Kenneth J. The Concept of Self. New York: Holt,
1971 Rinehart & Winston, Inc., 1971.

Gibby, Robert, Sr. and Robert Gabler. "The Self-Concept
1967 of Negro and White Children," Journal of Clinical
Psychology, XXIII, 1967.

Goffman, Erving. The Presentation of Self in Everyday Life.
1959 New York: Doubleday Anchor Books, 1959.

_____. Stigma. Notes on the Management of
1963 Spoiled Identity. Englewood Cliffs, N. J.:
Prentice-Hall, Inc., 1963.

Goldschmid, Marcel L. Black Americans and White Racism.
1970 New York: Holt, Rinehart & Winston, Inc., 1970.

Goodman, Mary E. "Evidence Concerning the Genesis of
1946 Interracial Attitudes," American Anthropologist,
N.S. XLVIII (1946), 624-630.

_____. Race Awareness in Young Children. New
1964 York: Collier Books, 1964.

Gordon, Chad. Looking Ahead: Self-Conceptions, Race and
1969   Family As Determinants of Adolescent Orientation
        to Achievement. The American Sociology Association,
        1722 N. Street, N. W. Washington, D.C., 1969.

_____. "Self-Conception and Social Achievement,"
1971   unpublished Ph.D. dissertation, University of
        California at Los Angeles. In Rosenberg and
        Simmons, Black and White Self-Esteem: The Urban
        School Child, 1971.

Gordon, Chad, and Kenneth J. Gergen. The Self in Social
1968   Interaction. New York: John Wiley & Sons, 1968.

Greenwald, H. J. and O. Oppenheim. "Reported Magnitude of
1968   Self-Misidentification Among Negro Children:
        Artifact?" Journal of Personality and Social
        Psychology, v. 8 (1968), 49-52.

Gregor, James A. and D. A. McPherson. "Racial Attitudes
1966   Among White and Negro Children in a Deep-South
        Standard Metropolitan Area," Journal of Social
        Psychology, LXVIII (1966), 95-106.

Grier, William H. and Price M. Cobbs. Black Rage. New
1968   York: Basic Books, Inc., 1968.

Grossack, Martin M. "Perceived Negro Group Belongingness
1954   and Social Rejection," Journal of Psychology, 1954.

_____. "Some Personality Characteristics of
1957   Southern Negro Students," Journal of Social
        Psychology, XLVI (1957), 125-131.

Grygenheim, F. "Self-Esteem and Achievement for White and
1969   Negro Children," Journal of Projective Techniques
        and Personality Assessment, v. 33 (1969), 63-71.

Gurin, Patricia, et al. "Internal-External Control in the
1969   Motivational Dynamics of Negro Youth," Journal of
        Social Issues, v. 25, No. 8, (Summer 1969), 29-51.

Gutterman, Stanley, editor. Black Psyche: The Model
1972   Personality Patterns of Black Americans. Berkeley,
        Calif.: Glendessary Press, 1972.

Haggstrom, Warren C. "Self-Esteem and Other Characteristics
1962   of Residentially Desegregated Negroes," Social
        Psychology, 3007-3008.

Hauser, Stuart T. Black and White Identity Formation.
    1971 New York: Wiley Interscience Division, John
          Wiley & Sons, 1971.

Heiss, Jerold and Susan Owens. "Self-Evaluations of
    1972 Blacks and Whites," American Journal of Sociology,
          v. 78, No. 2, 1972.

Helgerson, Evelyn. "The Relative Significance of Race,
    1943 Sex, and Facial Expression in Choice of Playmate
          by the Preschool Child," Journal of Negro
          Education, v. 12 (1943), 617-622.

Heller, Celia S. Structured Social Inequality. A Reader
    1969 in Comparative Social Stratification. London:
          MacMillan Co., 1969. [Selected readings.]

Henderson, E. H. and B. Long. "Personal-Social Correlates
    1971 of Academic Success Among Disadvantaged School
          Beginners," School Psychologist, 1971.

Herman, Melvin, et al. Study of the Meaning, Experience,
    1965 and Effects of the N.Y.C. on Negro Youth Who Are
          Seeking Work. New York: Center for the Study of
          Unemployed Youth, New York University Graduate
          School of Social Work, Part I, Chap. IX (1965),
          166-177.

Hodgkins, Benjamin J. and Robert G. Stakenas. "A Study of
    1969 Self-Concepts of Negro and White Youth in Segregated
          Environments," Institute for Social Research,
          Florida State University, 1968, Journal of Negro
          Education, v. 38, 1969.

Hollander, E. P. and Raymond G. Hunt. Current Perspectives
    1971 in Social Psychology. New York: Oxford University
          Press, 1971. [Parte II and III, selected readings.]

Horowitz, Ruth E. "Racial Aspects of Self-Identification
    1939 in Nursery School Children," Journal of Psychology,
          VII (1939), 91-99.

Hraba, Joseph. "The Doll Techniques: A Measure of Racial
    1972 Ethnocentrism?" Social Forces, L (June, 1972), 522-527.

Hunt, David E. and Robert H. Hardt. "The Effects of Upward
    1969 Bound Programs on the Attitudes, Motivation and
          Academic Achievements of Negro Students," Journal
          of Social Issues, XXV (Summer, 1969), 122-124.

Johnson, David W. "Freedom School Effectiveness: Changes
   1966 in Attitudes of Negro Children," Journal of
         Applied Behavioral Science, II (1966), 325-330.

Johnson, H. E. W. "The Relationship of The Self-Concept
   1970 of Negro and White College Freshman to The Nature
         of Their Written Work," North Texas State University,
         unpublished dissertation, 1970.

Kardiner, Abraham and Lionel Ovesey. The Mark of
   1951 Oppression. New York: Norton Press, 1951.

Katz, Irwin. "Review of Evidence Relating To Effects of
   1964 Desegregation on The Intellectual Performance
         of Negroes," American Psychologist, v. 19 (1964),
         381-399.

Keller, Suzanne. "The Social World of the Urban Slum
   1963 Child: Some Early Findings," American Journal of
         Orthopsychiatry, 33, (1963), 823-831.

Knowels, Louis and Kenneth Prewitt. Institutional Racism
   1969 in America. Englewood Cliffs, N. J.: Prentice-
         Hall, Inc., 1969.

Kohn, Melvin L. and Carmi Schooler. "Class, Occupation, and
   1969 Orientation," American Sociological Review, XXXIV
         (October, 1969), 659-678.

Kvaraceus, William, et al. Negro Self-Concepts. Implica-
   1965 tions for School and Citizenship. New York:
         McGraw Hill Book Co., 1965.

Landrath, C. and B. C. Johnson. "Young Children's Responses
   1953 to a Picture and Insert Test Designed to Reveal
         Reactions to Persons of Different Skin Color,"
         Child Development, 24 (1953), 63-80.

Larson, Richard, et al. "Kindergarden Racism," in
   1973 Comparative Studies of Blacks and Whites in the
         United States. Kent S. Miller and Ralph M.
         Droger, New York: Seminar Press, 1973.

Long, Barbara H. "Self-Esteem: A Self-Social Construct,"
   1969 Journal of Consulting Psychology, B. 33, no. 1,
         (1969), 84-95.

Lory, Barbara and E. H. Henderson. "Self-Social Concepts
   1968 of Disadvantaged School Beginners," Journal of
         Genetic Psychology, v. 113 (1968), 41-51.

Maliver, Bruce L. "Anti-Negro Bias Among Negro College
1965 Students," Journal of Personality and Social
Psychology, II (1965), 770-775.

Manis, Jerome G. and Meltzer, Bernard N. Symbolic Inter-
1967 action: A Reader in Social Psychology. Boston:
Allyn and Bacon Co., 1967. [Part I, art. 1;
Part 2, arts. 9, 12, 13, 14; Part 3, arts. 18,
19, 20, 21, 24, 25; Part 4, art. 29.]

Marx, Gary T. "The Psychological Context of Militancy,"
1972 in Black Psyche. The Model Personality Patterns
of Black Americans. Berkeley, California:
Glendessary Press, (1972), 191-214.

McDill, L. et al. "Sources of Educational Climate in
1966 High School," Department of Social Relations,
Johns Hopkins University, Final Report, Project
No. 1999, submitted to Bureau of Research, U.S.
Office of Education, Department of Health,
Education and Welfare, 1966.

McDonald, Robert L. and Malcolm D. Gynther. "MMPI Norms
1962 for Southern Adolescent Negroes," Journal of
Social Psychology, LVIII (1962), 277-282.

_____. "Relationship
1965 of Self and Ideal-Self Descriptions With Sex,
Race, and Class in Southern Adolescents," Journal
of Personal and Social Psychology, v. 1 (1965),
85-88.

McWhirt, R. A. "The Effects of Desegregation on Prejudice,
1967 Academic Aspiration, and The Self-Concept of
Tenth-Grade Students," Dissertation Abstracts,
v. 28 (1967), 2610-B.

Mead, George H. Mind, Self, and Society. Chicago:
1934 University of Chicago Press, 1934.

Meir, August and Elliott, Rudwick, editors. The Making of
1971 Black America. Studies in American Negro Life.
History and Sociology. New York: Atheneum, 1971.
[Vols. 1 and 2, selected readings.]

Merton, R. K. and A. Kitt. "Contributions to the Theory
1950 of Reference Group Behavior." Continuities in
Social Research: Studies in the Scope and Method
of 'The American Soldier'. Glencoe, Ill.: The
Free Press, 1950.

Meyers, Edna O. "Self-Concept, Family Structure And School
    1967   Achievement: A Study of Disadvantaged Negro Boys,"
           Dissertation Abstracts, 27 (1967-Sociology),
           3960-A.

Miller, Kent S. and Ralph M. Dreger. Comparative Studies
    1973   of Blacks and Whites in the United States. New
           York: Seminar Press, 1973.

Milner, Murray M. The Illusion of Equality. New York:
    1973   Jossey-Bass, 1973.

Moreland, J. Kenneth. "A Comparison of Race Awareness in
    1966   Northern and Southern Children," American Journal
           of Orthopsychiatry, 36 (1966), 23-31.

_____. Racial Attitudes in School Children:
    1972   From Kindergarten Through High School. U.S.
           Department of Health, Education and Welfare.
           Office of Education. Washington, D.C., 1972.

_____. "Racial Acceptance and Preference of
    1961   Nursery School Children in a Southern City,"
           Merrill-Palmer Quarterly, 8 (1961), 271-280.

_____. "Racial Recognition by Nursery School
    1958   Children in Lynchburg, Virginia," Social Forces, 39
           (1958-59), 132-137.

Mussen, Paul H. "Differences Between the TAT Responses of
    1953   Negro and White Boys," Journal of Consulting
           Psychology, XVII, No. 5 (1953), 373-376.

Noel, Donald L. The Origins of American Slavery and Racism.
    1972   Columbus, Ohio: C. E. Merrill Publishing Co., 1972.

Parker, Seymour and Robert Kleiner. "Status, Position,
    1970   Mobility and Ethnic Identification of the Negro,"
           in Black Americans and White Racism, Marcel L.
           Goldschmid, editor. New York: Holt, Rinehart
           and Winston, Inc., 1970.

Pettigrew, Thomas F. Racially Separate or Together? New
    1971   York: McGraw-Hill, 1971.

Powell, Gloria and Marielle Fuller. Black Monday's Children.
    1973   New York: Appelton Century-Crafts, 1973.

_____. "School Desegregation
    1970   and Self-Concept," Paper Presented at the 47th
           Annual Meeting of the American Orthopsychiatric
           Association in San Francisco, California, March 23-
           26, 1970. Also in Rosenberg and Simmons, op cit.

Radke, Marian J. and Helen G. Trager. "Children's Perceptions
    1950 or the Social Roles of Negroes and Whites,"
          Journal of Psychology, XXIX (1950), 3-33.

Radke, Marian, Helen G. Trager and Hadassah Davis.
    1949 "Social Perceptions and Attitudes of Children,"
          Genetic Psychology Monographs, 40 (1949), 327-447.

Radke, Marian, Jean Sutherland, and Pearl Rosenberg.
    1950 "Racial Attitudes of Children," Sociometry, XIII
          (1950).

Rainwater, Lee. "Crucible of Identity," in Black Psyche;
    1972 The Modal Personality Patterns of Black Americans.
          Guterman, Stanley S., editor. Berkeley,
          California: The Glendessary Press, Inc., 1972.

Roback, Howard. "Human Figure Drawings: Their Utility in
    1968 the Clinical Psychologist's Armamentarium for
          Personality Assessment," Psychological Bulletin,
          v. 70, no. 1, (July, 1968), 1-19.

Rohrer, John and Munro S. Edmonson. The Eighth Generation
    1960 Grows Up. New York: Harper and Row, 1960.

Rosenberg, Morris. "Race, Ethnicity and Self-Esteem," in
    1972 Black Psyche; The Modal Personality Patterns of
          Black Americans. Stanley S. Guterman, editor.
          Berkeley, California: The Glendessary Press,
          Inc., 1972.

Rosenberg, Morris and Roberta G. Simmons. Black and White
    1971 Self-Esteem: The Urban School Child. The Arnold
          and Caroline Rose Monograph Series in Ecology.
          Washington, D.C.: American Sociological Association.

Roth, Rodney W. "The Effects of 'Black Studies' on Negro
    1972 Fifth-Grade Students," in Banks and Grambs,
          Black Self-Concept. New York: McGraw-Hill
          Co., 1972.

Seeman, Melvin. "Skin Color Values in Three All-Negro
    1946 School Classes," American Sociological Review,
          (1946), 315-321.

Segal, Bernard. "Racial Perspectives and Attitudes Among
    1966 Negro and White Delinquent Boys," Phylon, XXIX
          (1966), 27-39.

Simmons, Roberta G. "The Experimentally Increased Salience
1968- of Extreme Comparative Reference Groups,"
1969 Sociology and Social Research, v. 53, 1968-69.

Simmons, Roberta G. and Morris Rosenberg. "Functions of
1971 Children's Perceptions of the Stratification
Systems," American Sociological Review, v. 36,
nos. 1-3 (1971), 235-249.

Soares, Anthony T. and L. M. Soares. "Self-Perceptions
1969 of Culturally Disadvantaged Children," American
Education Research Journal, v. 6, no. 1 (1969),
31-45.

Stevenson, H. W. and E. C. Stewart. "Developmental Study
1958 of Race Awareness in Young Children," Child
Development, XXIX (1958), 399-409.

Swensen, Clifford. "Empirical Evaluations of Human Figure
1968 Drawings: 1957-1966," Psychological Bulletin,
v. 70, no. 1, (1968), 20-44.

Taylor, Charlotte P. "Some Changes In Self-Concept In The
1968 First Year of Desegregated Schooling," Dissertation
Abstracts, v. 29 (1968), 821-A.

Trager, Helen G. and Marian K. Yarrow. They Learn What
1952 They Live. New York: Harper & Brothers, 1952.

Trent, Richard D. "The Relation Between Expressed Self-
1957 Acceptance and Expressed Attitudes Toward Negroes
and Whites Among Negro Children," The Journal of
Genetic Psychology, 91 (1957), 25-31.

Warner, W. Lloyd, et al. Color and Human Nature. Negro
1969 Personality Development in a Northern City. New
York: Harper Torchbooks, 1969.

Wayne, Dennis. "Racial Changes in Negro Drawings," Journal
1968 of Psychology, v. 69 (1968), 129-130.

Wendland, Marilyn M. "Self-Concept in Southern Negro and
1967 White Adolescents as Related to Rural-Urban
Residence," unpublished Ph.D. dissertation,
University of North Carolina, 1967.

White, William F. and Bert O. Richmond. "Perception of
1970 Self and of Peers by Economically Deprived Black
and Advantaged White Fifth-Graders," Perceptual
and Motor Skills, XXX (1970), 533-534.

Williams, R. L. and Harry Byars. "The Effect of Academic
    1970   Integration on the Self-Esteem of Southern Negro
           Students," Journal of Social Psychology, v. 80
           (1970), 183-188.

_____. "Negro Self-Esteem in a
    1968   Transitional Society," Personnel and Guidance
           Journal, XLVII (1968), 120-125.

Woodward, C. Vann. The Strange Career of Jim Crow. London:
    1966   Oxford University Press, 1966.

Works, Ernest. "Residence in Integrated and Segregated
    1971   Housing and Improvement in Self-Concepts of Negroes,"
           American Journal of Sociology, LXVII (July, 1971),
           47-52.

Wylie, R. C. and E. B. Hutchins. "Schoolwork-Ability.
    1967   Estimates and Aspirations As A Function of
           Socioeconomic Level, Race and Sex," Psychological
           Reports, v. 21 (1967), 781-808.

Yancey, William L., et al. "Social Position and Self-
    1972   Evaluation: The Relative Importance of Race,"
           American Journal of Sociology, LXXVIII, no. 2
           (1972), 338-359.

Yeatts, Pearline. "An Analysis of Developmental Changes
    1967   In The Self-Report of Negro and White Children,"
           Dissertation Abstracts, v. 21 (1967), 823-A.